THE BEST DEVOTIONS OF

Sheila Walsh

WOMEN OF FAITH™

THE BEST DEVOTIONS OF

Sheila Walsh

ZONDERVAN™

GRAND RAPIDS, MICHIGAN 49530

ZONDERVAN™

The Best Devotions of Sheila Walsh
Copyright © 2001 by Sheila Walsh

Requests for information should be addressed to:

Zondervan, *Grand Rapids, Michigan 49530*

Library of Congress Cataloging-in-Publication Data

Walsh, Sheila, 1956–
    The best devotions of Sheila Walsh / Sheila Walsh.
       p. cm.
    ISBN: 0-310-24172-3
       1. Meditations.   2. Christian life.   3. Walsh, Sheila, 1956–
I. Title.
BV4832.3 .W35 2001
242—dc21   2001026809

Published in association with the literary agency of Alive Communications, Inc., 7680 Goddard Street, Suite 200, Colorado Springs, CO 80920.

Interior design by Beth Shagene

Printed in the United States of America

01 02 03 04 05 06 07 08 /❖ DC/ 10 9 8 7 6 5 4 3 2 1

With love to my mother, Elizabeth Walsh,
and to my sister, Frances Burns
Your love and support
have always meant the world to me

Contents

Foreword by Marilyn Meberg

"Y ou realize that's the last Earl Gray tea bag . . . are you sure you want to take it?"

Sheila looked at me with a deadpan expression and said, "I have complete peace about taking the last bag."

"Of course that leaves me with only an English Breakfast tea bag, and it's four o' clock in the afternoon. I'm not sure I can drink breakfast tea in the afternoon." With an unmistakable twinkle, Sheila said, "I guess you'll find out, won't you?"

That was my first conversation with Sheila four years ago. I loved her immediately. We were meeting for a planning session for the *Women of Faith Bible*, but I was also aware she was the new addition to our speaking team. Within minutes there was no doubt in my mind what a fantastic decision it was to invite her on board. She made insightful comments during our meeting, tinged frequently with that Scottish droll that delighted me.

With the passage of time and shared experiences, it was apparent to me we could "do damage" together. For instance, during the singing in one of our Chicago conferences, I leaned over to Sheila and said, "I'll give you fifty dollars if at some point while I'm speaking, you just come up on the platform and start picking lint out of the carpet."

"Do I say anything?"

"No, just busy yourself with lint picking."

"How long do I pick?"

"A few minutes."

She didn't respond; however, a few minutes into my speech I turned and saw Sheila on the opposite end of the stage, hunkered over picking lint. Then wordlessly, she turned and went back to her chair and sat down.

I, of course, couldn't maintain my composure and had to tell everyone that little stunt cost me fifty bucks.

However, Sheila doesn't need anyone else to help her "do damage." One of my favorite stories illustrating her off-the-wall irrepressible humor was when years ago in England she found herself bored to tears listening to the endless pontificating of a man speaking to an audience of people who also found themselves sinking into a collective coma. Because Sheila provided the music for the event, she was backstage. Thinking she'd get a breath of fresh air she opened the stage door and found a friendly dog wandering around in the alley. It took very little encouragement for him to wiggle-bottom his way over to her. Scooping him up she brought him backstage with her. He was a wonderful diversion but Sheila felt selfish in keeping the diversion to herself. After all, the audience needed a diversion too, so she parted the stage curtain and the dog went bounding out. He leaped on the speaker's legs, barked at the audience, and ran in enthusiastic circles. After a few minutes of this delicious reprieve, Sheila dashed out as a self-appointed heroine, picked up the happy dog, and delivered him back to the alley. The audience was charmed, the speaker befuddled, and Sheila, of course, innocent of all questionable behavior.

This fun-loving dimension of Sheila is fully apparent as she mothers her darling son, Christian. They laugh, play, and most recently lay on their stomachs in the backyard staring intently at the "bug life" in the grass. In spite of her good looks and glamorous image, grass stains don't phase her, especially if she and Christian get them together.

It is not just Sheila's incomparable humor that charms me but her genuine faith as well. I have a hard time relating to piety expressed in hackneyed spiritual clichés, which cause me to wonder what's real and what's merely practiced. Sheila is real; I love to hear her pray. She prays her heart concerns without a touch of "churchiness" that reflects her straightforward confidence in the Father's love and acceptance of her. She is as she is.

You will find that same authentic flavor in her writings. One of my favorite devotionals in this book is "Out of the Shadows." In it she talks about her experience with clinical depression and the liberating influence it has had on scores of women as Sheila has dared to talk about the subject. She says, "I used to be more concerned with being spiritual than with being real, but I now sense that people in pain need to know that they are not alone in their struggles; we need each other to be real." I say a hearty nonchurchy amen to that!

So now, may I invite you to draw your chair up to the fire, pour a cup of tea, and prepare to have your soul enriched, your spirit touched, and on occasion, your funny bone tickled as you enjoy *The Best Devotions of Sheila Walsh*.

Vision

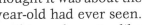

For when [King] David had served God's purpose
in his own generation, he fell asleep.
ACTS 13:36

One year my summer job was working behind the haberdashery counter of the largest department store in town. It took me a while to become familiar with all the stock. We had roll upon roll of ribbon, boxes of buttons, zippers, cotton thread, pretty handkerchiefs, and one very strange item.

I came across it one day when business was slow and my boss told me to clean out all the drawers. It had obviously been some time since they had been cleaned, and I spent most of the day rerolling ribbon and putting buttons into little boxes. The item was in the bottom drawer. I pulled it out and dusted it off and thought, *What a stupid thing. No one wants one like that.* I dusted it off and put it back in the drawer, convinced it would never sell.

When Miss Ferguson came back from her afternoon tea break, she asked me how my task was progressing. I showed her all the clean drawers, the neat rows of ribbon, and the boxes of buttons. I didn't mention the item in the bottom drawer. Perhaps she had ordered it. It was hardly my place to tell her that I thought it was about the stupidest thing that this sixteen-year-old had ever seen. The trouble is that I can never leave things alone. I'm like a terrier who buries a bone in the yard and digs it up every twenty minutes to see if it's still there. I couldn't contain myself:

"Miss Ferguson," I began, "we have only one of those items in the bottom drawer."

"Oh, I know," she said. "We sold so many in May and June."

You have got to be kidding! I thought.

She continued. "I'm sure we had at least twenty at the beginning of the summer. You can imagine how popular they are with our young ladies."

"You mean girls buy these?" I asked incredulously.

"Of course, dear, who else?"

"Well, I wouldn't want one," I said doggedly.

"Oh, they all say that, but someday you will," she replied with a smile.

"Miss Ferguson, I don't mean to be rude, but what would I want with a lacy plunger?"

Miss Ferguson, who was in her seventies, looked as if she were about to choke.

"A what?" she cried.

"A lacy plunger," I said. "It's not very practical and the lace will get wet when you stick it in the sink."

"My dear child," she said with tears rolling down her cheeks, "this is for bridal bouquets. You arrange the flowers in the top and you carry it by the white handle decorated with lace."

I could have died. By the next day the "lacy plunger" story was all over the store. Salespeople can be merciless!

How wrong I had been in miscalculating this item's purpose. One verse buried in the Acts of the apostles refers to King David, who "served God's purpose in his own generation." Christ too was so clear in the purpose of his life. His mission statement was well defined. Do you and I know why we are here, what we have been made for, our purpose? Sometimes we live out what other people perceive as our vision and calling and never discover for ourselves what that really is. Sometimes we are afraid to reach out and live the life that we believe we have been called to. But fear is no friend. It may seem to protect, but it slowly suffocates.

Someone recently asked me if I could state in a sentence what my life is all about. I replied, "The purpose of my life is to learn to love God more and to communicate that love and grace to others." That is why I am on the planet. When you know what your mission statement is, life is so much easier; you become free to line up your activities, relationships, and goals with that stated intent. What is your place in the kingdom of God? If I were to ask you to give me a sentence that encapsulated your vision for your life, what would it be? David discovered his purpose and fulfilled it in his generation, and so must we. Otherwise, you and I could be using our lives to clean sinks, when we were made for so much more!

Be thou my vision, O Lord of my heart;
Naught be all else to me, save that thou art:
Thou my best thought, by day or by night,
Waking or sleeping, thy presence my light.
ANCIENT IRISH PRAYER, TRANS. BY MARY BYRNE

Heaven Celebrates Our Birth

Immediately, something like scales fell from Saul's eyes,
and he could see again.
ACTS 9:18

I picked up my Bible and sat on the sofa waiting for my mother and sister to change clothes. With the impatience of an eleven-year-old, I drummed my fingers on the arm of the sofa.

I was excited about this evening's concert. I had never heard a gospel group before. They were called The Heralds, and they were from Edinburgh. The event was held in the local movie theater, which meant that the seats were more comfortable than church, and I hoped the candy station would be open.

But it wasn't. No smell of popcorn filled the air. *The folks who organized this event blew it!* I thought. *Christians eat a lot.*

We sat behind another family from our church. The daughter, Rosalind, was one of my best friends.

When the group was introduced, I could not take my eyes off the trombone player's red pants. It was like watching a London bus jumping around onstage. The musicians were very good, and I looked around the theater to see if any of my friends from school were there. I had invited several of my classmates who didn't go to church, and I was hoping that this evening would touch them.

After about an hour of music, a man stepped to the center mike and introduced himself as Ian Leitch. He talked about the love of God. I craned my neck to see if one particular boy in my class was "getting it," when Ian said something that made me snap back and pay attention.

"God has no grandchildren, only sons and daughters. Just because your parents go to church does not mean that you have a relationship with God by osmosis."

"What's *osmosis*?" I whispered to my mom.

"It means that you can't absorb it," she said. "You need to choose for yourself."

I was devastated. My nice little safe church world suddenly seemed like a very drafty place. As he continued, it became clear to me that I was not a Christian. I was hardly ever out of church, but I was not a Christian. I had never invited Christ into my life. I began to shake as tears rolled down my cheeks. Ian invited people to come to the stage if they wanted to surrender their lives to Christ. I couldn't move. Suddenly Rosalind got up out of her seat and walked to the front of the theater. My heart was pounding, my head was pounding, but I could not move. It was as if my legs had melted into a river, and I knew that they would not hold me up. I watched as people streamed to the front. I saw the boy from my class at school go forward and I cried even more. I thought that he needed God, but now he would be part of the family and I would not. The concert came to a close and everyone began to leave. I noticed that my mother reached over and hugged Rosalind's mother.

As we rode the bus home, Ian's words played over and over in my head. A huge struggle was going on inside me. I was afraid. The picture presented that evening had been overwhelming. It made the flannel graphs and action choruses in Sunday school seem trivial. It was clear to me now: Being a Christian was not a hobby. It was giving God all of your life.

I got ready for bed and kissed Mom good night. I tried to sleep, but the very air around me seemed charged with the anticipation of my response. God had spoken my name and I had to reply. I got out of bed and went back downstairs. "Mom, can you give your life to Christ only in a meeting, or would it be possible at home?"

My mother reassured me that God listens to our prayers wherever we are. So that evening, when I was eleven years old, as my mother prayed with me and led me to the door of the kingdom, my life changed forever. I was young, but I understood clearly that this was the most important thing that would ever happen to me, even if I lived to be a hundred. I lay awake for hours, feeling more alive than ever. I had no idea what my life would be like, but I knew that it would be forever.

The Holy Spirit may have moved differently in your life. For some it is a slow process of coming to faith; for others it is a sudden confrontation on the road. But for all of us—when we are called from death to life, when we discover what we were really made for, heaven celebrates our birth.

Behind the things we see and feel,
beyond the reach of what seems real,
a deeper thirst calls us by name;
and turning to that sweet refrain,
our eyes behold you, Lamb of God,
and running now o'er well-worn sod
we quench our thirst in Thee.
Amen.

Soul to Soul

Be merciful to me, O LORD, for I am in distress;
my eyes grow weak with sorrow,
my soul and my body with grief.
PSALM 31:9

It was a breezeless day with the hot sun beating down on the sticky tarmac. I had accepted an invitation to sing in a women's prison in Texas and the band was setting up on the blacktop. A few women gathered around, lighting up their cigarettes and making suggestive comments. I thought they were directed toward the guys in the band until the warden informed me that I was the topic of their conversation. The warden had brought in some additional security from the male prison a few miles away. Stepping to the mike, it was hard to ignore the guards with guns. They looked particularly sour because they had to stand out in the blazing sun listening to a Scottish Pollyanna sing about God's love.

I looked into the eyes of these incarcerated women as I sang, and I wondered if anything I had to say came close to touching the world they lived in. The warden had filled me in on some of their backgrounds and the crimes that had brought them behind these walls. Murder, manslaughter, and child abuse. I knew nothing of this world. They stared back at me as if I were from a mythical planet where life was as you'd always hoped it could be as a child. *How can I reach them?* I wondered.

Then I had an idea. I asked my lead guitarist, a mean blues player, to take the stage. As he allowed his instrument to sing out the song of the lost and lonely, I saw the women draw close. "Amen, brother," someone shouted, as she swayed to the heartbreaking melody that filled the air. There were no words, but no words were needed. Words would have been a hindrance because every story was different—but every heart, every soul, was the same.

I sat on the edge of the stage, captivated by the music and the women's faces as tears poured down their cheeks. There was a connection. It was soul to soul. The melody flowed behind the anger, the fear, and the defenses of us all, and it witnessed to the ache to be loved and accepted. For a moment it was as if the rain from heaven quenched the thirst in all of us to be heard, to be seen. I will never forget that day. I saw that beyond the choices we make for our lives, some good and some that lead us down the path of destruction, there is a common bond. It is our eternal nature, our soul.

So what is the soul? It is the deepest aspect of ourselves, the spiritual part that cries out for heaven, that is made to be a dwelling place for God. Nothing and no one else can answer that thirst. It is the size of eternity.

The longing filled the room.
It hung in the sticky air like a fly
   caught in a paper trap
suspended in its frailty.
Our thirst was for you.
It was for you we wept.
For a moment all walls came down
all voices were stilled
As God in Christ walked prison halls
   and spoke to us by name.
Thank you.
Amen.

When You've Lost Your Thirst

I will pour water on him who is thirsty.
ISAIAH 44:3 NKJV

I usually take care of my car, but a few months ago I was so busy training our new golden retriever puppy and doing some library research that I ignored the odometer that indicated an oil change was, well, overdue. My car seemed to be fine and I promised myself that I would do it "next week."

Then when I was pumping gas one day, an eager attendant asked if he could check my oil. He disappeared under the hood, and when he reappeared, he gazed at me as if I were a child molester. He held up a rod, black with sticky gunk.

I got the message, and the next day I dropped my car off for an oil change. When I picked it up, I could not believe the difference. It was as if I was driving a new vehicle. I had become so used to its sluggish behavior that I had forgotten how well my car can perform—if it's taken care of.

I see my soul as being like my car. As a vehicle needs clean oil, I need intimate contact with God. Our souls were made for this. When we deprive our souls of that very life force, we can survive—but that is all we are doing. We were not created to merely survive but to thrive in God.

This is a constant struggle for me. I am very headstrong and independent. Even though I know I need that intimate communion that settles my soul, I still run on blindly at times, not willing to stop and get the refreshment that would revitalize my whole being.

Sometimes we know we need refreshment but are too lazy in the routine of life — or too preoccupied with what we think is "important" — to stop for spiritual replenishment. Sometimes life may crowd in on us enough that we simply are not aware of our need. Think of the need for intimacy with God in terms of physical thirst. In the routine demands and distractions of the day, we can forget this most basic of all needs. I notice that on a hot day my dog, Bentley, is always returning to his water bowl for a drink. We might be playing with his ball, but at regular intervals he heads off for more water. Sometimes it's only in watching him that I realize how thirsty I am; I have the beginnings of a headache caused by dehydration. It's not wise to wait to change the oil when your car is running on treacle. It's not wise to wait to drink a glass of water after the headache is so bad you have to go and lie down in a dark room.

It is the same in our relationship with God. We can run through our days ignoring our need for him — intentionally or unintentionally — until we find ourselves dry and worn out.

If you sense you have lost touch with a thirst for God, talk to him about it. There is no glory in pretending and no shame in admitting what is true. Start with an honest confession to God that you have been distracted or negligent. Thank him for reminding you of your need — your thirst. We have forgotten how well we were meant to run.

Create in me a thirst, Lord,
that only you can fill.
Take this broken fragile life
this stubborn selfish will.
Renew in me a thirst for you.
My heart is dry and cold.
Break through the earth, a spirit birth.
Dear Lord, restore my soul.

A Thirst for Community

Now you are the body of Christ,
and each one of you is a part of it.
1 CORINTHIANS 12:27

When the Church wakes again it will know that
there can be no consequential change in the lives of people
unless there is community.
ELIZABETH O'CONNOR, *OUR MANY SELVES*

I have always viewed the psalms as intimate, deeply per-sonal prayers and songs. But it seems the psalms were liturgical poems used for corporate worship. They were read and sung aloud as a statement of faith of the people of God.

That communal purpose points out the huge obsession we in American Christianity have with self-discovery. In communal worship there is an accountability that does not allow us voyeuristically to point a finger at the world or the church; communal worship says we are part of the problem and are called to be part of the solution. That is one of the reasons I would like to live in a small town.

It seems to me that as a Christian this is all I need in life as I walk with God: a small group of people to live along-side, to learn from, to disagree with, to be changed by.

I used to love big cities and big malls, but I think maybe really I liked the anonymity of being able to disappear in such a setting and be accountable to no one. I cannot change on my own. I have tried and it doesn't work. I need to rub up against others to have my rough edges smoothed away.

Last night my husband, Barry, and I went to see a movie with friends — *The Spitfire Grill*. What I loved about it was the accountability of small-town life. Everyone knew each other, and the events of every family touched everyone else.

The town in the movie was called Gilead. The meaning was clear. There is a balm in Gilead. There is healing in community. The town was full of characters, the nosy postmistress, the insecure judgmental husband, the intimidated wife, the broken Vietnam veteran. The townsfolk frequently clashed, but on one level that was good news, because in that process they were forced to look at themselves; in that process they were given an opportunity to change. If that husband and wife, for example, had lived in a big city where their relationship was hidden behind high walls of anonymity, I'm sure they eventually would have become a divorce statistic. If the war veteran had lived in a heartless city, he would have slipped into obscurity, one more bum to give a wide berth to on the street corner. But they all lived in a cauldron of a little town that caused them to be seen as they really were.

That is what the church is supposed to be like. So often these days we hide within the walls of large churches. We come in as strangers and we leave the same way. We smile at one another, give the impression that we are the one family that has it all together, and go home to our private wars. Life was not meant to be that cold. We need each other so badly. Respectability is a thin coat on a winter's day. It is better to be known with all our hypocrisy and failings. We are the body of Christ, and deep inside each of us is a thirst to be known and loved, to be part of the stream of life. As we sing the psalms together, we see ourselves and each other and yet we see our frailties within the context of the grace and mercy of God.

We can't all pack up and head for some mythical town in Maine, hoping that within the space of a two-hour movie our lives will have taken on more meaning. But we can all begin to change how we live. We can start a small group in our home where we commit to grow together. We can be more real and present in our families. We can take our eyes off ourselves and our own journey and realize that this is a group outing—that we are not supposed to arrive in heaven alone but hand in hand.

Called to love with hearts as strong
 and deep as rivers run,
Called to live beyond ourselves,
 beyond the webs we've spun,
Called to laugh with those who laugh,
 to cry, to weep, to sing,
to give ourselves, to live an offering.
Amen.

Wait for God

What can a man give in exchange for his soul?
MARK 8:37

All human love bears within it the seed of betrayal; it is a failure of love. No one knows that more than Judas Iscariot, that notorious betrayer who was quickly overwhelmed by the horror of his dastardly deed—but his remorse receives little press. Here's the gospel account:

> When Judas, who had betrayed him, saw that Jesus was condemned, he was seized with remorse and returned the thirty silver coins to the chief priests and the elders. "I have sinned," he said, "for I have betrayed innocent blood."
>
> MATTHEW 27:3–4

What lay under that act of betrayal? Perhaps a deep thirst to right all wrongs now, to grasp hold of justice with his own two hands and pull it into his world. I see Judas's life as one that spoke of impatience. I see a deep thirst for more than the life he had lived as a young man. I imagine him leaving his father's vineyards in Kerioth, frustrated and restless; this farm life was not for him. There had to be more. He wanted Christ to act in ways that made sense to him. He wanted a savior of his own molding. Deep within his soul he was thirsty for a different life, but he wasn't willing to wait for the "something more" Christ would offer.

Even in the end, after the betrayal, Judas could not hold on. Now he stood with the rope in his hands, clenching the tool that would end his miserable life. His heart thundered in his ears, his stomach retched. What a fool he had been. His mind treated him to a picture show of a thousand memories that had brought him to this moment. He thought of his father, of boyhood friends, but he felt he couldn't go to them; none of them would understand what he had done. He had no choice but to end a life that had tipped the first domino for someone else. He could not bear to think of Jesus now. He could not bring himself to watch what he had participated in. He threw the rope over a sturdy branch.

But if he had waited three more days he would have seen Christ risen from the dead.

When we abandon ourselves to hopelessness we remove ourselves from Christ, our only hope — like the lemmings, who hurl themselves from a cliff into the sea. If only Judas could have held on a little longer. As Ray Anderson writes in his book on the life of Judas: "At the same moment that Judas is enacting the human drama of sin and death, Jesus is enacting the divine drama of redemption and atonement."

Augustine said that our hearts are restless until they rest in God, but we try all sorts of things to still that pounding in our heads and the ache in our souls. For some, it is the promise of success and what that golden cloak will feel like. For others it is the frantic, futile search for that one person who will fully understand us and make us whole. For Judas? Perhaps a chip on his shoulder and a desire for power that would make him feel like he was someone to reckon with.

There is no doubt that what he did was the ultimate act of betrayal, but I think of the words of Jesus on the cross: "Father, forgive them, for they do not know what they are doing" (Luke 23:34). I wonder if Judas was one of the people on his mind.

Our impatience to have God move now, to act in ways that make sense to us, will drive us to take control of our lives. God is moving in ways that we cannot see or understand. This means we are left with the question, "Do I trust him?" We can choose to bow the knee now and ask him to forgive us for trying to squeeze the answer we want out of heaven, or we will bow the knee later in remorse at our foolishness in thinking that we knew better than God.

We are all thirsty in different ways, deep down in our souls. It is a thirst as ancient as the hills. But it is a thirst that can be satisfied only in Christ.

Lord,
Forgive us for our impatience.
In our restlessness give us peace.
In our impatience give us hope.
In our thirst for you refresh us, we pray.
Amen.

Never Alone

The LORD himself goes before you and will be with you;
he will never leave you nor forsake you.
Do not be afraid; do not be discouraged.
DEUTERONOMY 31:8

I was in Bangkok, preparing for an evening concert at
the largest university in the city. I was the guest of
Youth With A Mission and Campus Crusade. My friends
from YWAM, Steve and Marie Goode, told me this was the
first time they had been able to organize a concert within
these hallowed walls, and they were excited about what
God would do.

"Tonight is a first," Steve said. "Bangkok is a hard city
to penetrate spiritually. The people are very religious, but
much of their religion is based on fear."

I thought of all the little houses, like dollhouses, that
I saw suspended outside restaurants and stores and asked
him about those. "Those are spirit houses," he told me.
"The people believe that if they build a home for the evil
spirits to live in, then the spirits will not come and live in
the people themselves."

"How awful to live in such fear and uncertainty," I said.

Steve told me that he anticipated a lot of spiritual war-
fare and trouble during the concert but that there would
be a continuous prayer meeting all evening. I naively
thought he was being overly dramatic; after all it was just

a concert. I was used to being in Britain or America where there is a certain receptivity to the Gospel, where years of prayer have soaked the soil. But in Thailand, Buddhism held sway.

As I stood at the microphone for a sound check before they opened the doors, I heard a strange scraping noise and turned to my right just in time to see a large heavy "tree" of stage lights come crashing down. I jumped out of the way as they smashed on the floor right where I had been standing. I couldn't believe it. No one had been near them to jar or bump them. There was no wind in the building. For the first time that night, I began to take Steve's words to heart.

I was delighted that a large crowd of students came. (The advertisements said that I was a pop singer from London, and British music was very popular in Bangkok.)

Before the concert began, Steve said, "We will be right behind you, just behind the curtain. We will be lifting you up in prayer every moment. God loves these students and it's time that they heard about that."

I was a little nervous, but as we prayed together before we went onstage, someone read these words: "The LORD himself goes before you and will be with you; he will never leave you nor forsake you. Do not be afraid; do not be discouraged." And for the next two hours I had to cling to that promise.

Halfway through the first song, the sound system went off and the second set of stage lights failed. There I was, standing in the dark, with no amplification. But my sponsoring team seemed prepared to jump any hurdle. I ended up singing through a bullhorn with a flashlight lighting up my face!

The amazing thing was what God did that night. Out of perhaps three thousand students more than half stayed behind to hear more about Jesus. And it certainly wasn't because they were impressed with the pop singer from London!

God is faithful to his Word. There are promises that he gives us that are surer than the blood that runs in our veins. When God says "never" it means never, not ever. We may find ourselves in places or circumstances that some would call "God-forsaken," but when we are there with him, he is there with us. That is a promise!

In the darkest place on earth he is there.
Where no other shadows rest he is there.
If you fall and bruise your heart,
Just remember this one part,
He is there.
He is there.
He is there.
Amen.

Never More Than You Can Bear

No temptation has seized you except what is common to man.
And God is faithful; he will not let you be tempted
beyond what you can bear.
But when you are tempted, he will also
provide a way out so that you can stand up under it.
1 CORINTHIANS 10:13

As Christians one of the greatest temptations we face is to quit. As I travel and meet people all over the country I hear more tales of discouragement than of blatant sin. Perhaps it is the legacy of some teaching that was popular in the seventies and eighties, when we were told that God wanted us to be healthy, wealthy, and wise. If we just had enough faith, a Mercedes would be parked in our driveway, our loving children would be serving God in perfect obedience, and any physical sickness would be a thing of the past. It sounded so wonderful.

I remember a discussion with a dear friend who had embraced this teaching wholeheartedly. I asked him how he would respond spiritually if one of his three lively daughters fell off a swing and broke her leg. He felt that if he had enough faith, his daughter would not fall off a swing. We talked long into the night about what faith really is. We parted as friends, but we were miles apart in our views. I soon moved away, and we didn't see each other for several years. Then we met again, both of us ministering at the same conference. I asked after the children, knowing that their lives would have moved on by leaps and bounds. Over a cup of coffee he told me about the changes in their lives.

"I thought it was going to break her mother's heart," he began. "I just wanted to kill the guy! I couldn't believe that my little girl was pregnant."

I listened as he told me about the cold wind that had blown through their home. The pregnant daughter wanted to be with the father of her child, and my friend and his wife were so against it. Great barriers developed in the family as they all retreated to their separate corners to cope with this crisis.

"All my nice neat theories went out the window," he said. "I thought I had it all tied up. I thought I understood God, but I was wrong."

"So what happened?" I asked him.

"For a while I couldn't pray," he said. "I could hardly talk to my wife or my children. I just wanted to give up. Nothing made sense to me anymore."

"But you're here today," I said. "I've just heard you sing, and I noticed a depth and a tenderness that were never there before."

"Well," he continued, "I came to the end of myself, which was very hard for me. I was a proud man, but I had to throw myself on God and tell him I couldn't take any more. And then he slowly began to rebuild me. It felt as if I were starting all over. All I knew was that Jesus loved me and he loved my wife and he loved my daughter and he loved the baby, and, most difficult of all, he loved the baby's father. Just when it seemed that this thing would destroy us all, God stepped in."

It's hard to let go of things in which we have placed our hope—even when they lie broken in our hands. It's even harder to let go of our preconceived ideas of how God works when those lie shattered at our feet.

Many of us carry around a heavy weight of discouragement. It seems as if nothing will ever get any better, nothing will change. In the midst of that I offer these words of hope, of promise: "God is faithful; he will not let you be tempted beyond what you can bear."

Perhaps it seems to you that you are at the breaking point. I urge you in the name of the Lord to throw yourself on him, to hide yourself under his wings. Don't give up. You have come too far. The road ahead may look bleak, but trust in God. It is the way home.

Dear Lord,
I bring myself before you now.
I lay this discouragement at your feet.
I lay the broken pieces of my plans before you.
I rest in you.
Amen.

I Almost Missed the Miracle

He answered: " 'Love the Lord your God with all your heart
and with all your soul and with all your strength and with all
your mind'; and, 'Love your neighbor as yourself.' "

LUKE 10:27

When I was seventeen years old, I worked for part of a summer at Hansel Village, a home for mentally and physically handicapped adults. On my first morning of work I was nervous as I got off the bus and walked to the main house. I had never spent time with anyone disabled, and I didn't know how I would react to the residents or they to me. At lunch the matron introduced me to the community, explaining that I would be helping out for a few weeks. A young woman with Down's syndrome immediately walked up to me, put her arms around me, and gave me a bear hug. The others took her cue. I stood there for about ten minutes as, one after another, they approached and hugged me. It was overwhelming. During my stay there I encountered a different kind of love than I had known before. It was childlike and pure. It was freely given and based on nothing but a shared joy and love of life. At night I would bring out my guitar and we would sing for an hour. One or two of the men would sit at my feet and my bear-hug friend would lay her head on my lap.

I remember one day in particular. We set off early for a nature walk and picnic lunch. Elizabeth, one of the residents, walked through the woods with her head down, looking at the ground. Afraid she would bump into a tree, I asked her what she was doing.

"I'm looking for a flower," she said.

Our path was strewn with wildflowers, so I figured she was looking for one particular flower. When I asked, she told me the name of it and what it looked like. She invited me to join the search.

"You'll never find it!" one of the young men cried. "She's been looking for it for months."

After lunch most of us caught a nap, lying on the grass or leaning against the trunk of an oak tree. But not Elizabeth; her search continued. When it was time to head home, we gathered up our belongings. Just then Elizabeth came running, skipping, and dancing toward me. "I found it! I found it! I found it!" she cried, joy splashed across her face as she held the tiny bloom in her hand.

Later that evening when all the residents were asleep I wandered up to my room. There on my pillow was Elizabeth's flower — the fruit of her long search — with a short note. "To Aunt Sheila with love, your friend for always, Elizabeth."

I carry that memory and those faces with me to this day.

This is what the church is supposed to look like. How can we love God with everything and our neighbor as ourselves if we do not sacrificially give of ourselves with joy? In looking for the big opportunities to "perform" as a Christian, how many small God-given opportunities to love with depth do we miss? How many small gifts are given to us that we don't even notice — because we're waiting for the big gestures?

This year I am asking myself a new set of soulful questions:

"Do I love God more this year than last?"
"Am I more compassionate and tender?"
"Am I allowing others into my life?"
"Is the fruit of the Spirit growing in me?"
"Am I taking risks for Jesus?"

Jesus' twofold commandment to love God and others as ourselves calls for a depth of love that I do not yet know. But in the midst of my discouragement there is a strong candle burning. I have more real friends now than I have ever had. We speak the truth to each other and keep walking together. These vital life lessons cannot be learned in obscurity and isolation. They are learned in community as we are forced to face ourselves as we really are and love enough to want to change. Life lived on the edge is tough and yet full of joy. I hold those Hansel Village summer memories as some of the richest of my life. For a few weeks I found friendship and acceptance based simply on the fact that I was a fellow human being. The residents of the community did not care what I would "make" of my life, they didn't think about "grand opportunities," they simply handed out the love of God, trusting that I would receive it and give it back in return.

I almost missed the miracle.
I tried to hurry by.
Wrapped up in an old box,
unappealing to the eye,
deep inside that package
what a true gift I was given
for some of God's most broken ones
are very close to heaven.
Thank you, Lord. Amen.

The Friendship of Books

I devoted myself to study and to explore
by wisdom all that is done under heaven.
ECCLESIASTES 1:13

Many of my best friends have more than two hundred pages! I have loved books since I was a child. I love to read and I still love to have books read to me. As Christmas approaches, Barry and I dig into our Christmas book box and read to one another. On alternating nights we take turns picking a story; we light a fire, sit back, and read or listen as we are carried away by *A Child's Christmas in Wales* by Dylan Thomas, *A Christmas Carol* by Charles Dickens, or the story of the Bethlehem birth.

Recently I was looking for a book to give to a friend. Glancing through shelf upon shelf of books I realized how many old friends I have. I noted *Hind's Feet on High Places* by Hannah Hurnard. When I was a student at London Bible College, that book helped chart me through some very difficult waters. I dusted off my collection of the works of Isaac Bashevis Singer and Thomas Hardy; both had enlarged my understanding of human nature. I picked up one of many volumes of poetry and read again the wonderful poem of Rudyard Kipling titled "If." I looked at the stiff binding of *War and Peace* and wondered why I've never been able to wade my way through it. My C. S. Lewis library is right on the front shelf; different books of his have touched me at various seasons of life. I love *The Lion, the Witch and the Wardrobe.* I love his poetry; I love *Surprised by Joy* and *The Screwtape Letters,* but my favorite of all is *Till We Have Faces,* a Greek myth retold.

So many books have influenced me. I love television and movies, but for me nothing will ever take the place of a good book. I have learned from the wisdom and folly of real and fictional characters. I have shed tears with weeping poets and laughed aloud at humorous or joyous scenarios. When I am sad or discouraged, I can pick up a book, find a quiet corner, and be reminded by the author of who I am in Christ. When I am being selfish or cold, a book can touch my heart and melt me to my knees.

I love to study the lives of men and women of faith who have gone before me. The light of their stories still shines, challenging me to live a life worthy of the calling of Christ. I pray that what I learn from the lives of others will be used by God to make me a more compassionate woman, more willing to serve, more grateful to God and of more use to others.

Sometime, when you feel a little lonely, consider a visit to your local bookstore. Ask a trusted friend to recommend a book that will lighten your spirit, deepen your wisdom, or widen your vision.

Find a new friend—in a book.

There are friends waiting on every shelf!

Lord,
Thank you that in a world without direction you have
left us signs along the way through the lives of those
who have gone before us or who walk beside us. Teach
us to hear your voice through them. Thank you for
good books that can be faithful friends and teachers.
Amen.

A Piece of Heaven

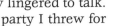

And when she finds it, she calls her friends
and neighbors together and says,
"Rejoice with me; I have found my lost coin."
LUKE 15:9

I was searching through my box of photographs to find a picture of our dog's first birthday party to send to my mom. (I had recently told her on the phone that Bentley wore a party hat and had a cake with candles; I wanted to back up this ridiculous assertion with physical evidence.)

Before I had unearthed Bentley's picture, I found three photographs that caught my attention. I made myself a cup of tea and sat outside in the shade to study them more closely. They captured three different occasions separated by some time. But many of the faces were the same.

The first one was a bridal shower that my friend Marlene threw for me. There were perhaps twenty women huddled together to get in the picture, laughing as we all tried to make sure our hair was unmussed and our skirts were straight. I thought back to that day and remembered that after all the laughter and silly games and cake, these friends gathered around me and prayed for Barry and me. After most of the women left, a few lingered to talk.

The second was a surprise birthday party I threw for Barry. I rented a karaoke machine, which was a huge mistake. Barry found one tape that was in his key and sang

"Rhinestone Cowboy" over and over until we all wanted to put a bullet through the speakers! The photo showed friends watching Barry and laughing as he tried to give Glen Campbell a run for his money. I remembered that after most people had gone home, a few of us sat around the fire, drinking coffee and talking about our lives.

The third was taken at our home, not long ago. Barry decided to honor the fact that I was turning forty and pregnant. On my birthday when I came home from an afternoon out with a couple of my close friends, I found thirty-five people in the house — with gifts for me and for the little one.

I looked at these photographs and thought again of how rich I am. On each occasion after the larger crowd had left, a few of us lingered around the fire for several hours. I thought of the words of C. S. Lewis: "Is there any pleasure on earth as great as a circle of Christian friends by a fire?" Each of my close friends brings something different to me. Barry is always making me laugh; he is so honest and real. Marlene, keenly aware of global concerns, "takes us" around the world and reminds us of the church in other countries. Frank draws us back to Scripture and holds the Word up as a plumb line to our ideas. Cindy is a straight arrow whose passion for purity flies straight and true. Sara's commitment to integrity and compassion cuts through our wordy rhetoric. Dan's love of books spreads a feast before us. Marilyn's warm and generous heart welcomes us all, and Steve's quiet wisdom anchors us. We are richer together than we are apart. Because of what each person brings, our lives are deepened and our vision enlarged.

C. S. Lewis said that we picture lovers face-to-face but friends side-by-side; I think that is even more true when Christ is at the center of our lives — when we are all heading in the same direction with one heart and mind, to become more like Christ.

I can survive without a lot of things, but to live without friends would be to live in a cave and never see the sunrise again. We need the input, the challenge, the encouragement, even the "spur" that comes from others in community. We call on each other to celebrate and we call on each other to weep. Surely this is a treasure above others, a piece of heaven, a promise of what is to come.

I see in you a piece of heaven never seen before.
I laugh with you and celebrate the good things
    at your door.
I weep with you when sorrow lays its hand upon
    your head.
And I am rich beyond this life for those whom
    I call friend.
Amen.

Practice Makes Perfect Peace

The LORD is my shepherd, I shall not be in want.
He makes me lie down in green pastures,
he leads me beside quiet waters.

PSALM 23:1–2

Good morning, Sheila. My name is Al."

"Good morning. I hope you had a good breakfast," I said making a halfhearted attempt at humor.

"I have a strong stomach."

This was my first driving lesson — at age twenty-seven! After my father died we didn't have a car. We rode the bus. As a newlywed Mom had tried to learn to drive, but because Dad — the teacher — was fiercely protective of his vehicles, I don't think she received much encouragement.

Driving looked so easy. I sat in the driver's seat and surveyed all the bells and whistles that one had to master to get a license; I listened as Al talked me through lesson one. Then came the big moment, turning the engine on. I felt like James Bond behind the wheel of an Aston Martin as I edged the car out of its parking space. We were on a quiet street in Costa Mesa, California, when Al made his first big mistake.

"You can go a little faster than this," he said.

"Hold onto your hat, Al!" I replied, as I lived out my Indy 500 dreams.

Halfway through the lesson Al asked if we could stop for coffee. I thought this was his normal practice. But as he sat in the coffee shop fanning himself with the menu, I wondered if I was a bit too much for Al.

It amazed me—how difficult it was to get it all right. It looked easy, but trying to get my hands to do what my brain was telling them at the right time—this was very hard.

"Will you be my instructor all the time?" I asked as we headed back to the car.

"Afraid so. I mean, yes," he said.

I remember thinking that I would never get it right; it would never come naturally to me, but I was wrong. All it took was consistent practice and commitment—and a few unscheduled coffee stops for Al.

A similar discipline is required in solitude. It is a learned discipline. Our environment offers any number of noisy options to keep us constantly entertained. We have forgotten how to be quiet. When I first began to give myself to the discipline of solitude I despaired of ever being able to quiet my mind. I would turn the radio or TV off and sit for a while. My mind would wander all over the place. I found myself thinking about what I could make for dinner, and did Lou Anne's carrot soup recipe call for one or two leeks? I was repeatedly discouraged, wanting to quit, reasoning that this was simply not the way for me to fellowship with God. But I didn't give up. I kept trying. After a while I began to relax into being alone with God. I left all my lists and requests behind. This was time for quiet, not for petition.

My times of silence before God are very important to me now. I put everything else down, every word away, and I am with the Lord. When I'm quiet, life falls into perspective for me. I have a very active mind and I'm a worrier, but in those moments when I choose to put that away, I rest beside the Shepherd in still places.

Why don't you give yourself a gift today? Turn off the television or the car stereo, put down the newspaper or the business plan, and in the quietness, rest for a while beside the Shepherd of your soul.

The only sound that visits me
is the rapid whir of wings,
a hummingbird caught in the air.
I turn from other things
to rest in you; you quieten me.
I lay my burdens down,
and by the river's edge I sit
dressed in a silent gown.
Amen.

Small Harbors

He who dwells in the shelter of the Most High
will rest in the shadow of the Almighty.
PSALM 91:1

Generally these days, when I go on a retreat, I travel some distance and am one of the guest speakers. In my teens and twenties I often gathered with a small group, enjoying the intensity of a few days together on retreat, most often out of town. Now I find "small harbors" as often as I can. By this I mean that instead of setting off on big trips, I have a lot of little departures. I find them in my day. I'm driving to the airport, and my car becomes a little harbor for quiet fellowship with God. I'm walking the dog, and as he sets off across the hillside I find a "small harbor" and sit down for a while. There is something very settling about a harbor; it steadies the boat.

A few years ago I was asked to go to Belfast, Northern Ireland, to perform a concert with my band. We sailed from Stranraer on the west coast of Scotland to Larne on the Irish coast. Despite the horror that Belfast has seen with bombings and riots, it is a beautiful city and its people have great hearts.

After the concert, as we sat in Larne harbor waiting for the boat to leave, we were all talking about the successful event and how much we enjoyed the people. It had taken me a long time to convince my saxophone player that he would be safe on this trip, but now that it was over and we were leaving, it was obvious to us all that we were carrying away a great memory.

Suddenly an announcement informed us that a storm had blown up; our boat would be the last one out that day. The captain gave a few other instructions about safety measures and then we set sail. Sitting in the harbor it was hard to believe that there was much trouble brewing, but once we were in the open sea, it was a different matter altogether. The boat began to tip from side to side. Dishes from the dining room were flying all over the place. Two of the band members were hanging over the side — rather the worse for wear. The crossing lasted only about an hour but there were many green faces as we docked in Stranraer. Once in that harbor it was quiet again, and the roller-coaster sea trip seemed unreal.

Harbors are like that. They give you a little shelter, a break in the maelstrom of the rough waters.

We don't always have time for grand departures to wonderful retreats or resorts where we can be refreshed and renewed. That is why I treasure small harbors. They are all around us waiting to let us catch our breath before the next wind carries us away.

Resting in you, Lord Jesus,
safe from the storms at sea,
tucked in your arms and sheltered,
here you will steady me.
Amen.

Still Enough to Hear

On my bed I remember you;
I think of you through the watches of the night.
PSALM 63:6

One of my greatest vices is that I talk before I think. (I remember the words of a godly counselor who told me the world would be a better place if I could cut in half what I had to say.) I have opinions on everything and love to give them regular airings. I process information very quickly and am ready to respond almost immediately, but I am slowly learning the benefit of taking time to meditate, to really listen, and to be changed by what I hear.

I think we in the church community have become shy of meditation because of our horror of all things that sound like the New Age movement. But meditation is a spiritual discipline, a gift to the church, that we as the people of God have been called to. In the book *The Way to Freedom,* I've read that when Dietrich Bonhoeffer was asked why he meditated he responded simply, "Because I am a Christian."

Consider the words of Psalm 48:9: "Within your temple, O God, we meditate on your unfailing love."

In *The Imitation of Christ,* Thomas à Kempis describes meditation as "a familiar friendship with Jesus." I like that. He talks about the end results of meditation—being able to hear God's voice and obey his word. "A familiar friendship" evolves as we spend time with someone—not just talking but watching and listening, observing how that person reacts, learning what he or she likes and doesn't like. A familiar and strong bond builds between two people. You know your friend very well.

A simple example comes to mind. Recently Barry and I were flying back to Los Angeles after an exhausting trip. Our flight had been delayed four hours in Chicago. By the time we finally took off on the last leg home, we were bone tired and we hadn't eaten in hours. Then we were stuck right at the back of the plane—where people lean on you as they wait to use the rest room! By the time the flight attendant got to us with the meals, she was out of what Barry wanted. Frustrated, he gave up and said he didn't want anything to eat, thank you.

I thought about this for a moment and then asked if we could please have his meal. When that tray was put down in front of him, he smiled at me and said, "You know me so well"—meaning I knew he was really hungry but just too tired to shift in his mind and accept a meal that wasn't his first choice; I knew he needed to—wanted to—eat.

I know Barry so well because I've spent so much time with him. And I get to know God as I spend time with him, meditating on his Word. Meditating on the Word of God is a very different discipline than reading the Bible or praying. When I meditate, I take perhaps just one verse and sit with it for a while and ask God to speak to me. I might keep it in my mind for the whole day.

Consider the verse "Perfect love casts out fear" (1 John 4:18 NKJV). It immediately speaks to me. But as I sit with it for a long time, so much more comes to my heart. I ask, "What is perfect love?" I think about my own fears and what it is like to let God's love touch them and take them away. As I sit with God I experience a new level of intimacy and worship, a deeper confidence and trust in him.

Mary, the mother of Jesus, accepted the angel's message to her and pondered his words in her heart. That is meditation—to reflect or consider with thoroughness and care. God's Word is life to us and yet we spend so little time truly taking it in.

As we meditate on God's Word, we become familiar with God's heart and his ways; as we do so, we will change. The purpose of meditation is not simply to make us feel good in a noisy world; it is not a self-absorbed agenda. Rather, as we shut our mind in with God and reflect on his words, we will know him and be changed by him—and that is the purpose of our lives.

"Be still, and know that I am God."

Lord, grant me the stillness of heart and mind that I will know you in ways deeper than I have ever known you before. Amen.

Be Still

Be still, and know that I am God.
PSALM 46:10

In my second trimester of pregnancy I experienced severe shortness of breath. My doctor referred me to a pulmonary specialist, who arranged for tests. "I've scheduled you for noninvasive venous studies—this afternoon," he said. "They will detect any blood clots in your legs. If we find anything, I'll have you admitted right away."

As I lay on the hospital bed waiting for the technician to begin the tests, my mind started racing:

"Did I leave enough food out for the dog?"

"I should have picked up Barry's shirts from the dry cleaners yesterday."

"I'm starving."

"I have a speaking engagement this weekend. I can't be in the hospital."

I looked at the machines around me and wondered what this day had in store. Then I listened to the sounds coming from the room next door. Sitting in the waiting room, I'd seen the patient going in. She seemed to be in severe pain. Her husband helped her with every labored step.

Now, from next door, I could hear an ultrasound machine. As it scanned, it amplified the sound of blood pouring through veins and arteries. The sound—like the ocean on an angry day—was unnerving as it washed into the quiet of my room. I closed my eyes. When I opened them again they rested on a poster on the wall in front of me. It said, "We carry within us the wonders we seek without us."

I was struck by the simple beauty and truth of those words. How often had I looked outside of myself for peace and joy and intimacy in my relationship with Christ, as if it were a gift that someone else might give me? We think that if we just read the right book or attend the right conference or travel to the church where everyone says that God is showing up in unprecedented ways, then we will find that wonder—that joy—we are seeking. But I have discovered this is not true. That joy and peace that we go off hunting for are always experienced secondhand. We have a divine gift through the sacrifice of Christ; this means we can come directly into the presence of God by ourselves. True joy does not lie outside of us. It is not at the end of a telephone line or a new job offer or a new partner; it lies in the stillness of our moments with Christ.

I thought about the woman in the next room. Her blood is always pumping in her veins, but she can't hear it; it is a hidden world. Only when she lies in a quiet room with the world tuned out and a special machine turned on does the unheard world that is always there become the most present thing. So it is with Christ. That is the gift of solitude. When we get away from the invasive noise and activity of this world that makes so many demands on our time and attention, when we tune into our relationship with Christ, we discover the wonder that we are waiting for. We can wait for wonder to come knocking at our door. But if we will be quiet and listen, we will hear it knocking at our hearts.

Dear Lord,
In the stillness I wait for you;
in the stillness you wait for me,
for there I will know in my soul,
in the depths of my heart,
that you alone are God. Amen.

Standing Alone Together

Now you are the body of Christ,
and each one of you is a part of it.
1 CORINTHIANS 12:27

In *Letters and Papers from Prison,* the German theologian Dietrich Bonhoeffer wrote, "Let him who cannot be alone beware of community."

I have thought about this interesting statement for some time. At first it seemed contradictory. Surely it is the lonely who need to be in community. But I now see Bonhoeffer's point. Those who cannot be alone with themselves expect others to be their lives, and no one can do that for another human being.

There are so many weak, malnourished believers who have never grown in Christ. What happens when they are in community? You have a roomful of needy children who are expecting someone else to help them make it through this life, who have no skills to enable them to resolve conflict and nothing to give to others. I believe that is what Bonhoeffer warns about.

We are all called to stand up and be who we are in Christ. That is something that we find out on our own with the Lord. God will use others to help us, but each one of us came into this world alone and we will all stand alone before God when we die.

Standing alone is vital for our spiritual health. We are urged to pray for one another but that does not mean that we abdicate our individual commitment to pray for ourselves. When we, by ourselves, know who we are in Christ, when we have a strong personal relationship with him, then we have so much to offer each other.

Sometimes we want to step in and rescue a fellow believer from any discomfort that may come in the maturing process. But I'm reminded of an insight I've learned from nature. Baby birds can die when someone steps up and cracks open the eggs at hatching time. The birds need the pecking and effort, which gives them fortitude. The struggle builds into them what they will need to survive in the world; outside interference — though well intentioned — can write a death certificate for the birds.

I used to think that I could carry a few of my more wounded sisters over the finishing line, but I realize now what a disservice that is. It is not love. We are not called to take each other's burdens away; we are called to share that burden, to walk alongside. We are called to encourage one another to keep our eyes on Jesus, the author and finisher of our faith.

As we stand alone with Christ and receive from him, we are able to be part of a living, growing community of faith. Drawing our strength from him in solitude, we can know who we are and what he has called us to, and we can bring that with us each time we are together — as fellow members of the body of Christ. How rich a life — as individuals and as a community — that would be.

From that first cry as we are broken into the world
  we are alone.
At that last sigh as we make our journey home
  we are alone.
Teach us, Lord, to stand alone so that
  we can stand together. Amen.

For God Alone

Therefore, I urge you, brothers, in view of God's mercy,
to offer your bodies as living sacrifices, holy and pleasing
to God—this is your spiritual act of worship.
ROMANS 12:1

In the New Testament we are called to be *living* sacrifices. That's in contrast to the *dead* sacrifices of the Old Testament, where a young animal would be killed. After its blood was drained, it would be offered up to God as a sacrifice. A slain animal no longer has a choice, but you and I do. Think about it: A living sacrifice can crawl back off the altar if it gets too hot. It requires a daily choice to stay on that altar no matter how intense the heat.

Paul says that, in view of God's mercy, we should offer our lives to him in a way that costs us. True love involves sacrifice. That is where discipline comes in. Sometimes I don't feel like praying or opening my Bible. And at times I have reasoned that because I am free in Christ, under grace not law, it is okay for me to slack off and not push it.

But then I think of my relationship with my husband. I am sure there are days when he comes home, feeling too tired—after a long workday and a long drive—to talk to me or be loving or kind. But he chooses to. Some days after sitting at my computer all day, I'll look at the clock and realize that I'd better get a move on to fix dinner and fix myself before Barry comes home. I could think, "Oh well, he's my husband; he'll understand that I'm too busy to take care of that." But that would be foolish and selfish behavior. Because he loves me, he gives himself to me even when he is tired; I know at times it's a sacrifice. Because I love him, I give myself to him; and yes, sometimes it's a sacrifice. (It's easier to look like Phyllis Diller on an off day.) Why would we offer anything less to the Lord?

It's easy to forget that we are called to bless God with our lives. We think that God is there to bless us; we think there should be some benefit to us at every moment. God does not exist just to make our lives better; we exist so that we can learn to love and worship him in spirit and in truth. Love that involves no sacrifice at all is not love; it is cannibalism, feasting on someone else for what we can get out of it.

Discipline has been a hard lesson for me to learn. It doesn't come naturally to me, but I have come to appreciate its gifts. I love to write. Some days when I sit down at my desk, the words flow so easily and it's pure joy. Some days I don't feel inspired at all, but I've learned the value of giving myself to my work anyway. At the end of a hard day, when I feel I have had to push myself through, I feel a tremendous satisfaction, knowing that I didn't waste the day. Similarly, when I give myself to worship when I would rather turn on the television or read a book, I often rejoice, realizing that these moments are some of the most special times I have with the Lord. As I pull my mind and heart away from myself and tune in to the greatness and goodness of God, my faith is matured. I delight in what is right and honorable. God is more than worthy of the disciplined offering of our lives. He never holds himself back from us, and when we give ourselves to him, we present worship with flesh on it, a gift with content, words undergirded by our lives.

"Therefore, I urge you, brothers, in view of God's mercy, to offer your bodies as living sacrifices, holy and pleasing to God—this is your spiritual act of worship."

Come before him now
offering your soul in worship
giving back the life he gives us
honoring the one who loves us.
Come before him now in worship
Holy is the Lord.
Amen.

Prayer Changes Things

If you remain in me and my words remain in you,
ask whatever you wish, and it will be given you.

JOHN 15:7

"Prayer changes things." That was the badge I wore on my jacket as a sixteen-year-old. I then viewed prayer as some type of external influence; we could align our hearts with God's heart and pray toward a change in a circumstance or person. But over the last few years I have discovered that what is most changed by prayer is the one who is praying. I see that prayer changes me. I can't stay the same when I pray. If I feel anger or resentment toward someone, I can't pray for that person and still hold on to the intensity of my emotion. Presenting a person or situation to God changes how I view it. I start with one stance, but as I spend time with God looking at the situation, I find that the world shifts a little. I'm given new perspective on what I see.

For two years I have had a hard time forgiving a friend who walked away from me when I really needed him. I couldn't understand why he was so distant and cold. I found it hard to pray for him; every time I tried to pray my feelings got in the way; I wanted him to know how much he had hurt me. I wanted him to hurt as he had hurt me. Yet I knew this was wrong, and my unforgiving spirit was affecting my life. And I kept thinking of the verse, "Anyone who claims to be in the light but hates his brother is still in the darkness" (1 John 2:9).

I felt stuck. My friend had no desire to be reconciled to me or to talk to me about the distance between us. I couldn't seem to throw off this "stone" that was dragging me down. So I began to seriously pray for him. I forgave him, not because I felt any forgiveness, but because Christ has forgiven me. I prayed that God would bless him and bring him closer to Christ every day. I prayed this for months. At times I would think I was making real progress, and then his name would be mentioned, maybe someone telling me that he had said something negative about me, and all the old feelings would come rushing back. But I would stop, grab hold of my heart, and pray for him again.

Over time I realized that God was changing my heart. I began to see this person as more than just the cause of hurt. I could remember his gifts and good qualities. He became a whole person in my mind again rather than just the perpetrator of one act. I still don't know if and when I will be reconciled with my friend, but I know that I am not the same person who began to pray for him two years ago.

Without the call to discipline I would have given up a long time ago. I would have seen our estrangement as his problem and attempted to move on in my life. But how can I remain in Christ and hate my brother? How can I expect God to hear and answer my prayers if I hold onto such a cold place in my heart? When I started to pray for him, my motive was that God would change him. That was my whole intent. As I continued in prayer with discipline as a dear and trusted friend, I saw that it is God's heart to change me.

If you feel stuck bring your whole self to Christ, not just the problem, but you. Ask God to change your heart.

Commit yourself to pray to that end. It's God's heart to give good gifts to his children.

Prayer, a gently crafted tool
chisels at my heart
working on the stony ground,
shaping me till love is found
where fear and anger lay.
Thank you, Lord, for the gift of prayer.
Amen.

Renew Your Mind

Do not conform any longer to the pattern of this world,
but be transformed by the renewing of your mind.
Then you will be able to test and approve what
God's will is—his good, pleasing and perfect will.
ROMANS 12:2

Fifty percent of your grade will be based on your research paper, which must be turned in two weeks before the end of the semester."

I sat in seminary class in church history and listened to Professor Nathan Feldmeth as I scanned the list of possible research topics. The paper had to be twenty-five pages long and include a bibliography of reference material.

For the next few nights I sat at my desk at home and wrestled with the task of writing this paper. Then, after the next class, I asked the professor if I could talk to him. "I don't know how to do this," I admitted.

"What do you mean?" he asked kindly.

"Well, I've never written a paper for a graduate class, and I honestly don't know where to start."

For thirty minutes Nate sat with me and went over each step: how to research, how to catalog the research, how the finished paper should look. He helped me understand how to access knowledge, how to read a book so that I will understand it, grasp hold of what is being said, and then determine if I agree with the writer. I left that meeting grateful for his guidance and guidelines. I felt less ignorant, more confident that I could take one step at a time.

In all of life, study is a faithful friend if we learn its ways. I see that a great deal of damage is done not by evil but by ignorance. Christ tells us that we will know the truth and the truth will set us free (John 8:32), but so often we don't know what the truth is. We don't know how to dig it out. In Romans Paul tells us that our lives are to be transformed by the renewing of our minds. But if we have no firm grasp on what God's Word says, how can we be changed by it?

I think we Christians have become lazy. We would rather read a book about how someone else became closer to God than spend time alone with him ourselves. We would rather listen to someone else's interpretation of the Word of God than read it for ourselves. And yet we alone are accountable for what we believe. We can't stand before God on the day of judgment and explain that our incredible ignorance is our pastor's fault. It is our responsibility to access God's Word for ourselves.

Think about how much damage is done by ignorance. So many marriages break up because the couple didn't have a clue how to communicate. Now, as I enter the final trimester of my pregnancy, I am keenly aware of parental responsibility. Though we are dismayed by many differing opinions on the right way to raise a child, Barry and I are reading all the how-to books we can — and then we will rely on God to guide us to make good choices.

Yes, study is a faithful friend if we will learn its disciplined ways.

As a Christian I am passionately committed to study. I want to know for myself what God says. I want to know the things that make him happy and the things that break his heart. I want to know how to live a life that will please him. How can I do that if I don't study his words to me?

There is nothing in life more important than understanding God's truth and being changed by it, so why are we so casual about accepting the popular theology of the moment without checking it out for ourselves? God has given us a mind so that we can learn and grow. As his people we have a great responsibility and wonderful privilege of growing in our understanding of him. If marriages could be saved and children's lives made richer by study and understanding and change, think of the impact on the church if we as individual Christians befriended the spiritual discipline of study.

I like to take a passage of Scripture or a good Christian book and write down what strikes me or what questions I have as I read. When I get together with my friends, I'll throw these thoughts into the arena and we'll wrestle with them to grasp hold of what God is saying to us. When we dig deep, there are hidden treasures to be found.

Your Word is like a flaming sword
A sharp and mighty arrow
A wedge that cleaves the rock;
That word can pierce through heart and marrow
Oh, send it forth o'er all the earth
To purge unrighteous leaven
And cleanse our hearts for heaven.

CARL GARVE

Foot Washing

After that, he poured water into a basin
and began to wash his disciples' feet, drying them
with the towel that was wrapped around him.
JOHN 13:5

In one great selfless act, as he got down on his knees
and washed the feet of his friends, Christ destroyed the
concept of what's "appropriate." If one followed the rules
of position and authority, he — the leader, the respected
teacher and miracle worker — was the last person in the
room who should have performed that menial task. In
the final few hours with his twelve disciples — men who
had been with him since the beginning of his ministry —
he delivered a powerful punch to what true greatness
really is.

We feel good about ourselves when others rush to
serve us; we are relieved when someone else volunteers
to do a job with no luster. Of all the patterns that Christ
modeled for us, this seems to be our least favorite.

I've worked with many people over the last twenty
years, and none has impressed me more in terms of
simple humility than Cliff Richard. Cliff is a huge star, a
household name in the rest of the world, although he is
not as well known here in the U.S. During his career he
has sold more singles than The Beatles, The Rolling

Stones, and The Who combined, and he is a very committed Christian.

I first met him, and was awed by his talent, on a charity tour for a British relief agency, Tear Fund. I was with the band that opened for him. Then his gospel manager, Bill Latham, became my manager and Cliff and I became friends. When Cliff coproduced an album for me, I was amazed at his attitude. He was there on time every morning and stayed until every session was over. He sang all the backup vocals to save me money and because he thought that it would be fun. For a while I was his regular opening act, and he always made sure that I had everything I needed. All this goes to say that there was nothing of the "star" about him in how he lived. He was a brother in Christ.

A few years later I invited him to the Christian Artists' seminar in Colorado. One morning as we were out walking, a girl came up and asked for my autograph. As I signed her book I introduced Cliff. She said, "Oh, great to meet you. You're Sheila's backup vocalist!" He just smiled and said, "That's right." At peace with who he was, he felt no need to remind anyone of his renowned role.

To my view, Cliff's humility stands in stark contrast to what I see in the church in America. We are very impressed with "gifting." And the art of giving, of serving, of servanthood is way down the list of valued qualities. We live in a culture that encourages us to alienate ourselves from people perceived to be "beneath" us. Or at best we patronize them, allowing them to serve us. But Christ says, "I have set you an example that you should do as I have done for you. I tell you the truth, no servant is greater than his master, nor is a messenger greater than the one who sent him. Now that you know these things, you will be blessed if you do them" (John 13:15–17).

To gain perspective, I suggest we turn back to the spiritual disciplines. As we pray and meditate and study and simplify our lives, we get a sharper picture of what is true and what is of worth and what is self-indulgent garbage. Spending disciplined time alone with God gives us a picture of our own worthlessness and the awesome majesty of who we serve.

Lord, give me the heart of a servant, to love without limit, to give expecting nothing in return, to wash the tired feet and tired hearts of those around me as you have washed my soul. Amen.

To Will One Thing

Therefore, as God's chosen people, holy and dearly loved,
clothe yourselves with compassion,
kindness, humility, gentleness and patience.
COLOSSIANS 3:12

I looked at the clock in my car and realized that I had ten minutes to make a fifteen-minute trip—and I was out of gas. I pulled into a station. As I got out of the car, a young attendant approached. "Good morning, ma'am. Would you like me to check your oil today?"

"No thanks, I'm kind of in a hurry." The sign said PAY BEFORE YOU PUMP. I thought I could save a few seconds, so I handed him a bill. "I want twenty dollars' worth. Would you take it in for me?"

"Sure would. It's going to be a hot one!" he said with a smile as he sauntered off at a snail's pace.

Oh man, I would have been quicker doing this myself, I thought. I watched as he stopped at another car to give someone directions, and by this time I was getting very frustrated. As the car pulled out, the guy turned and waved at me! I pointed to my watch.

"Yes, ma'am," he shouted.

Finally, when he'd paid the cashier, I lifted the pump to begin filling my car. He yelled at me to stop. "Hold up there," he said. "I'll be right over."

I ignored him and kept pumping my own gas. When he got to my car he reached over me and tried to take the pump from my hand.

"I've got it, thanks," I said.

"No, ma'am, that's my job. I'm here to serve," he said with a big puppy grin.

By this point I was really cross as he was trying to wrestle the pump out of my clenched fist.

"I've got it!" I said and pulled harder on my end.

"It's my job!" he cried and pulled back.

"This is a self-serve aisle!" I yelled.

"I know it is, but I'm helping!" he pleaded pitifully.

"You're not helping, you're making me crazy!" I told him.

At that point he wandered away muttering to himself, and I drove away very late and very frustrated.

That evening I couldn't get this young man's face out of my mind. I ran the whole scenario over and over in my head trying to justify my lack of patience: I was late and he was so insistent. "It's fine to offer to help, but you can't push yourself on people," I reasoned.

Then I thought of Paul's words: "Clothe yourselves with compassion, kindness, humility, gentleness and patience" (Col. 3:12).

I was so ashamed of myself. It is my expressed desire to live a life that demonstrates the love and compassion of Christ, but to that young man all I had exhibited was impatience and intolerance.

The next morning I drove past the gas station to see if he was there. I saw him on his hands and knees, polishing the bottom half of one of the pumps. I parked my car and walked over to him. "Do you remember me?" I asked.

He stopped what he was doing and looked up. "Sure I do," he said. "You're the lady who likes to pump her own gas."

"I'm here to ask you to forgive me for being so rude yesterday," I began. "You were trying to help me, and I was too stubborn to let you. I'm really sorry."

"That's okay," he said, as he stuck out his hand. "My name is James; I just like to do a good job."

I am still amazed at my lack of grace and kindness in the most simple of situations. I can go from speaking to a crowd about the love of God, feeling so close to heaven that it seems as if I have gold dust on my shoes to . . . driving in traffic and having someone cut me off—and I become a maniac.

All I know to do is (1) to keep bringing this rip in my soul to the foot of the cross and (2) whenever my unkindness touches the life of another to go to that person and ask forgiveness. It is my calling to treat every human being with grace and dignity, to treat every person, whether encountered in a palace or a gas station, as a life made in the image of God.

Breathe on me, breath of God,
Until my heart is pure,
Until with you I will one will,
To do and to endure.

EDWIN HATCH

To Grow We Have to Risk

In this way they will lay up treasure for themselves
as a firm foundation for the coming age,
so that they may take hold of the life that is truly life.
1 TIMOTHY 6:19

David sat at the bedside of a man whose breath was labored and shallow. The man stirred and opened his eyes. A nurse held a cup of water with a straw to the man's lips and then he turned his gaze to David, who introduced himself. "My name is David Pawson. I am chaplain here. Is there anything that I can do for you?"

The man stared at him and then laughed with energy he didn't have to spare. He coughed for a few moments.

"Shall I get the nurse?" David asked.

"No," the man replied. He looked at David intently. "Do you know who I am?"

Now David stared at him and said, "No, I am sorry; I don't recognize you. Have we met?"

"Hardly!" the man replied. "I am the president of the British Atheists Association."

"Do you want me to leave?" David asked.

"No. Stay awhile. I want to tell you why I don't believe in God."

David pulled his chair closer to the bed to make it easier for the man to speak.

"I don't believe in God because of you," he said bluntly.

"I don't understand," David responded. "Because of something I have done personally?"

"No," he replied. "Because of all of you. None of you believe what you say you believe."

"I still don't understand," David said.

The man pulled himself up in bed, and with all the energy and passion that was left in him, he looked directly into David's eyes. "If I believed what you all say that you believe, I would crawl over England on broken glass to tell people."

He sank back into his bed. The dialogue was over but those words of indictment were forever burned into the pastor's heart and soul.

Sometime later I met David at a conference. I was the singer and he was the guest speaker. As he told us this story, his voice caught when he related that dying man's final words to him; tears poured down David's cheeks. The words hung in the air. There was absolute silence in the room. We had spent almost an hour singing and rejoicing, celebrating God's love for us, but now the words of an atheist who spoke to us from the grave sobered us all. From the vantage point of the platform, I looked around the room and read the stories written on the faces in front of me. Some rolled their eyes as if to say, "What do you expect from a heathen?" Others shifted uncomfortably in their seats. Some were crying as they grasped the full impact of those words. I was devastated. I felt as shallow as a summer puddle after a short rain shower.

Think about it for a moment. We live in a desperate, decaying world, full of violence and hatred and fear. Every day teenagers take their lives because they see nothing to live for. In motel rooms all across our country, prostitutes give a little piece of their souls to men who don't even remember their faces. People drink and abuse drugs in an attempt to anesthetize their emotional pain and to try for a moment to stop thinking. We use and abuse each other in ways as old as our father Abraham. In the midst of all this chaos, there is a group of people, of whom I am one, who believe that there is hope written in letters as large as the Empire State Building: JESUS.

We know that there is more to this life than just getting through one more day. We actually believe that God loves us. We believe God's love was so intense that he sent his own Son to live among us — to show us what the Father is like and to die a brutal death in our place. We believe that whatever one's start in life, whatever mistakes one has made, there is forgiveness and a fresh start available. We believe that death is only the beginning of our real lives. We believe all of this, so why do we remain largely quiet about the Good News?

I am not suggesting that we stand out on the street corner and wave banners in the faces of passersby. I am suggesting that we invite the Lord to deepen our understanding of his love, to stretch our hearts and fill us till we are running over with the grace and compassion of Christ. Then we would take risks. Then we would reach beyond ourselves — and *that* would stand out. That would be different. That would be real. That might even cause an atheist on his deathbed to find his way home.

Father God,
Forgive me for the apathy of my life.
Forgive me for clutching your words of life to my
    chest like a life preserver
instead of throwing them out as a rope to the world.
Help me to live the words I believe,
to reach out beyond the comfort of my world,
to risk for you who risked all for me.
Amen.

Risking Everything

Stand firm in the faith; be men of courage; be strong.
1 CORINTHIANS 16:13

What matters is whether Christians will dare to risk
everything in order to fulfill their function in the world.
JACQUES ELLUL, *THE PRESENCE OF THE KINGDOM*

The house was quiet now, but the raised voices of the men who had carried her husband away still reverberated throughout the room. It took her some time to settle her six children and reassure them that God would be with their father tonight.

But when will I be with him again? she asked herself.

They had known for some time that they were in danger. Her husband, a dedicated pastor, had refused to bow to the Chinese authorities and surrender his house-church pulpit.

"How can I withhold the very words of life from those who need to hear?" he had asked her.

For so long she had feared a night like tonight. With no warning, a group of soldiers had burst into their quiet little home, charged the pastor with crimes against the government, and carried him away. It would be twenty-one years before she would see her husband again. That was his sentence, twenty-one years of hard labor in a prison miles from his family.

As she sat in the strange stillness of her room on that terrible night, she asked herself how she — alone — could possibly support six children. A short time later, the authorities made her an offer: If she would divorce and denounce her husband, they would take care of her and the children. She took a huge "risk" and refused.

To take such a leap of faith, you need to know who you are and what you were made for. You need to be confident that you are in the loving hands of the all-powerful God.

My friend Marlene recently had an opportunity to interview this saintly Chinese woman. In their eighties, she and her husband are now reunited, living in China, preaching the Gospel. Marlene asked her if she had ever been angry with God during those twenty-one long years.

The woman laughed. "Ah yes," she said. "I was very angry for about two weeks, and then the Lord told me not to worry. He told me that he had need of my husband, because there were many in prison who had never heard about Christ. I knew then," she continued, "that if God was taking care of him in prison, he would take care of the children and me; and he did."

I am in awe of people like this who risk all they have to remain true to who they are.

Whether or not we are ever called to show such courage and fortitude, we, like this brother and sister, can know without a shadow of a doubt who we are and whose we are. Knowing that, we can know why we are on this earth. That makes the rest of life fall into place — so that if we *are* called to take a stand for Christ — whether in a prison or an office building — our choice is made. We stand firm in our faith because it is our life.

Father God,
Today I lift up to you all those who suffer because they
hold your name up high. Give me the courage to hold
my standard strong whether in a howling gale or a
gentle breeze.
In Jesus' name,
Amen.

Out of the Shadows

Praise be to the God and Father of our Lord Jesus Christ,
the Father of compassion and the God of all comfort,
who comforts us in all our troubles, so that we can comfort
those in any trouble with the comfort we ourselves
have received from God.

2 CORINTHIANS 1:3–4

I must have just missed the call. I was out for only about twenty minutes taking Bentley for a run. When I returned I saw the familiar blink, blink on the answering machine and pressed the play button. "I just want to thank you for your book *Honestly*. I am a teacher who has been put on leave of absence and diagnosed with clinical depression. I felt so ashamed," the voice said. "I thought that I was the only one, you see. I didn't think that Christians suffered with this, and I felt so alone. I read your book, and I just want to say, God bless you for writing this. I know now that I'm not alone."

I listened to her voice and my heart went out to her. I said a prayer for her that God would be very close as she walks through this dark valley.

That call seemed important to the woman who left the message, but it also meant a lot to me. It brought home something that I strongly believe in. When I was considering writing *Honestly*, which dealt with my struggle with clinical depression, a couple of friends were concerned that some people would "not understand" and would dismiss me as some kind of nut, maybe pigeonhole me as the poster child for depression. I knew this was possible, but I also felt that we are called to take risks for one another, to stand beside those who are wounded, and to share the comfort we have received. There is such a stigma attached to any illness of the mind, and so many people suffer in silence, alone, afraid to admit that they are sinking a little more every day. I felt I should do what I could to break that silence and help others.

One particular occasion pushed me to write my story. I had been asked to speak at a women's prayer breakfast in Orange County, California. The organizing committee told me that I could talk about whatever was on my heart. I had never publicly talked about my hospitalization, and I hadn't arrived intending to do so. But as I looked out at that group of women, I felt moved to tell them where I had been and what God had done and was continuing to do in my life. As I talked I saw that tears streamed down many faces across the room. At the end of the morning I lingered and spoke with a few women who came up. I noticed a beautifully dressed woman hanging back a little, waiting for the crowd to thin out. Soon we were alone and we found a corner to sit and talk as the busboys cleared the tables.

"I haven't told anyone this," she said, "but I have suffered with depression for a year now. I have felt so ashamed and so alone. I cannot thank you . . ." She could not continue, and we sat for a while holding hands, two sisters who have shared so many similar struggles. Her face stayed with me and I wondered how many others there were like her . . . and so I wrote my book.

I used to be more concerned with being "inspirational" than with being real, but I now sense that people in pain need to know that they are not alone in their struggles; we need each other to be real. I am not advocating a coast-to-coast spiritual pity party. Rather, I suggest that as we receive the help and comfort of Christ, we in turn take a risk and extend that same hope and comfort to others. This is not a time to hide behind walls and put on a brave face; this is a time to stand in the light with our wounds and our flaws. Having taken that risk, we can encourage others to risk and come out of the shadows, find healing and find comfort in Christ. Those who reach out, who risk being known, will have the privilege of sharing the grace and mercy of God with others. (And believe me, there is a broken heart in every crowd.) That is what the family of God is all about.

Speak softly to the human heart
that hides behind a wall.
Speak words of life and comfort
from the greatest gift of all.
For every heart that's breaking
needs a touch from Christ alone,
so pour this oil
on arid soil;
speak softly to them all.

The Gift of Crisis

A certain ruler asked him, "Good teacher,
what must I do to inherit eternal life?" . . .

[Jesus] said to him, "You still lack one thing.
Sell everything you have and give to the poor, and you
will have treasure in heaven. Then come, follow me."

When he heard this, he became very sad,
because he was a man of great wealth.
Luke 18:18, 22–23

I love to listen to audio books. If I have a long drive the miles seem to melt away as Garrison Keillor takes me to Lake Wobegon or Meryl Streep reads *The Velveteen Rabbit*. On this particular day I had received a package of tapes in the mail from Pastor Bob Phillips.

I stopped at my usual coffee haunt for a cup of latte—to go—and put the first tape in the cassette player in my car. The message was about the young successful man who stopped to talk to Jesus to check that his spiritual life was as on track as his business portfolio.

The man didn't receive the answer he was hoping for. In fact he was told to take everything that was working for him and get rid of it, to strip himself of his very identity as a wealthy man. He was obviously a good man, a decent citizen. Why then was he asked to reduce himself to the ranks of the poor and destitute?

I used to puzzle over this story. Jesus must have encountered many wealthy people without requiring that they give everything away. Even Zacchaeus, who had cheated people all of his life, gave only half of his wealth to the poor (Luke 19:8). So why was Christ so hard on this man?

As I listened, Bob said something that made me turn off the tape and think for a long time. It was one of those *Eureka!* moments, when you know that what you just heard is very important. Bob said that Jesus created a crisis in this man's life to show the man what was within him. It really had nothing to do with the money per se; it's just that money was in this man's heart as an idol. With that insight the gospel story made sense.

What Christ cares about is our hearts, our complete love and devotion. And he will create crisis in our lives to show us what holds us.

I remember how devastated I was when I found myself in a psychiatric ward, suffering from clinical depression, with a career lying in tatters at my feet. At first glance my situation looked like the worst thing that could ever happen to me. But that was just the first look.

As I looked closer I began, slowly, to see that I had been given the most awesome gift, the gift of crisis, to see what was in my soul. Some of it was ugly. I saw fear and anger, pride and unforgiveness, but I also saw Christ there with open arms, inviting me to change. What a gift!

We don't need to view crisis as an enemy but as a friend. If we see that the whole purpose of life is to become more like Jesus, then crisis is indeed a gift, for as the weeds of our hearts are exposed, they can be uprooted. That is painful sometimes, but pain is very necessary if we want to grow.

The gospel account of the "rich young ruler" ends by saying that he went away sad and that Christ let him go. Jesus didn't run after him and say, "Okay, how about fifty percent?" Jesus let him walk away. What God is after in the darkest night of our souls is our whole heart, nothing less. If you find yourself in the midst of a crisis, stop for a moment and thank God, invite him into the crisis, and see what he will make of you.

Dear Lord,
Thank you that you love me enough to gift
  me with crisis.
I pray for courage that I will not fall back.
I pray for grace that I will not give in.
I pray for eyes to see you in the darkest
  moments of my life.
Amen.

Comfort

For just as the sufferings of Christ flow over into our lives,
so also through Christ our comfort overflows.

2 CORINTHIANS 1:5

In my hotel room I unpacked my case quickly and hung my suit for the next day's conference. I changed my watch from California to Detroit time and called Debbie.

"Hi, I'm here. Are you up for a visit?" I asked her.

"Are you kidding!" she replied. "Get yourself over here, now!"

I called down to the front desk and asked for a cab. As I rode about fifteen minutes over to my friend's house, I wondered what I would see when I got there. Debbie had tried to warn me that she did not look good and had deteriorated considerably since my last visit. I knew that the flesh on her right leg was all but gone, not only from the cancer, but also from the flesh-eating virus she had caught. I prayed, "Lord, please help me to be strong for Debbie." Since I was pregnant, my stomach was unreliable. Sometimes just fixing the dog's breakfast was enough to make me lose mine.

"Here we are, miss," the cab driver said.

Debbie's mom, Mildred, was at the front door, a smile warming up her tired face. We hugged each other and commented on how long it had been since we had last been together. Debbie's dad shook my hand. As I hugged her two sisters I could see my friend out of the corner of my eye, sitting in a wheelchair in the family den. I walked over and gave her a very gentle hug. Her right arm is broken but they can't put it in a cast because the extra weight would break her fragile shoulder.

"Hi, friend!" I said, as she grinned up at me.

"Well, you don't look very pregnant!" she said in mock indignation. "I thought you'd look like Shamu by now!"

"Any day now," I reassured her.

The family gathered round to share a pizza, and we caught up on each other's news. Then, as if by some unspoken signal, they all drifted off and left Debbie and me alone.

"So how are you really doing?" I asked.

"Not so good," she said. "I'm so tired. I don't think I can do this much longer. The pain never leaves and having the dressings changed on my wounds is more than I can bear. The cancer is spreading to new areas. I really don't know how I'm still alive."

I looked at my friend, wrapped in a decimated sixty-five-pound body, and I too did not know how it was possible that she was still alive. For years she has struggled. Of all the people I have encountered in my life, I know of no one who has suffered more than Debbie.

"How is this affecting your faith, Debbie?" I asked.

She sat for a moment in silence and then replied.

"I've actually lost a lot of faith," she told me, "faith in the things of this world. I've lost faith in all the silly things that we think are so important, all the stuff we do to impress each other, but my faith in Christ is stronger than ever."

"Help me understand that," I countered. "When you are in so much pain, where is Christ?"

"When I am rushed to the hospital again and I can't breathe and I'm bleeding internally and all around me is panic—at those moments it is as if Christ gathers me up into his arms and holds me. He is the only one who can hold me and not break anything."

I looked at my dear friend and knew that this was no Pollyanna. She was confirming what Paul told us: "Just as the sufferings of Christ flow over into our lives, so also through Christ our comfort overflows."

Debbie has asked me to conduct her funeral service, and I consider it to be one of the highest honors I could ever be given. It will not be a time of wailing for the end of something but a time of celebration for the home-coming of a saint of God who, in the darkest night of her life, held on to Jesus as he held on to her.

Her footprints are fewer than mine,
every one is executed at a high price;
some hardly make a mark,
like a feather descending onto snow.
But if you stop for a moment and
*   look at where they're going*
their path is very clear:
They're going home,
a straight line home.
You're almost home, my dear.
Amen.

Waiting in the Dark

He went away a second time and prayed,
"My Father, if it is not possible for this cup to be taken
away unless I drink it, may your will be done."
MATTHEW 26:42

I had never been angry with God. I'd found it hard to relate to others who had told me they struggled with this; it seemed so foreign to me — until recently. I was doing well in my pregnancy. Because I turned forty in my fourth month, I knew I was considered higher risk than some women, but I didn't give it much thought.

Based on intuition and guesswork, we were sure it was a girl and had chosen a name, Alexandra Elizabeth.

"Are you disappointed that it's not a boy?" I asked my husband.

"Absolutely not!" he said. "I just want a healthy baby."

At nineteen weeks I went for an ultrasound. Barry took the day off work, and we were so excited we didn't know what to do with ourselves. "Well, do you want to know the sex?" the nurse asked.

"Yeah, we'd love to!" we replied in unison.

"It's a healthy-looking boy."

I thought that Barry was going to hit his head on the ceiling. He let out a yell of delight and did some thanksgiving dance known only to men.

"I guess he's happy!" the nurse said, smiling at me. We left the hospital on cloud nine. I did a quick mental switch and realized that I was going to love being mom to a little boy; I'm not the froo-froo lace and ribbons type. We stopped on the way home and bought him five outfits and then called our families and shared our joy with them.

Two days later my doctor called. "Are you sitting down?" she said.

"Yes," I said. "What's wrong?"

"Your blood screening test came back and it doesn't look good," she explained. "I'd like to have you meet with a genetic counselor as soon as possible."

I knew what she was talking about. This was a test that screened for birth defects and was given routinely to women over thirty-five. I called Barry at work. He took the morning off and came with me. We walked into that waiting room as one sober couple. We didn't talk. We sat and held hands until they called my name. The counselor brought out charts and graphs and talked on and on, but I couldn't hear him. All I could hear was that something was wrong with our baby.

"I've made an appointment for you to have an amniocentesis at eleven o'clock," he said.

"Why would I do that?" I asked. "We're not going to abort the baby, no matter what the problem is."

"Well, that's your choice," he said. "But if the baby is very handicapped and your doctor knows that information, it will help in the delivery."

"How long will we have to wait for the results?" Barry asked.

"Ten days," he said.

Later, waiting for the test, I lay on the table with none of the joy that I had felt a few days ago. The nurse brought the baby's picture onto the screen so the doctor would not harm him when he put the needle into the amniotic sac. I looked at this little one wriggling around, full of life, and I had to turn my head away from Barry as the tears flowed down my face.

"This will hurt a little," the doctor said as he pushed the needle in and extracted two vials of fluid.

"Honey, whatever happens, the Lord will be with us, and I will be beside you every step of the way."

I looked at my husband and smiled, but inside I was a cauldron of emotions.

"Why don't you lie down for a while?" Barry said when we got home.

"The timing of this could not be worse," I said. I was leaving the next morning for a ten-day tour to promote my book *Honestly*. Barry would not be with me on the trip, so we would have to wait separately, me in Dallas and Barry at home.

For the first two days on the road, I was okay. I cried at times, but that seemed to give me some relief. Then an unfamiliar emotion surfaced, and I realized that I was angry at God.

"If this is supposed to be another test to make me a better Christian, then forget it. I don't want it that badly," I cried. "I'll stay the way I am."

I felt torn in two. I couldn't deny what I was feeling, and yet I felt ashamed of what I was feeling. What right did I have to demand a "perfect" child? And yet I wanted to make that demand. The waiting seemed the hardest part.

I imagined what life would be like, raising a handicapped child. "You're a hypocrite, Sheila," I told myself. "You tell people that the handicapped kids you used to work with were some of the most loving people you've ever known. You just don't want one of your own."

I didn't want to talk to God; I knew that I had to make my peace with him about whatever was going to happen, but I didn't want to.

This struggle went on for a week. Then, on the seventh day, I was in Marion, Illinois, for a TV interview. By early afternoon it was over. I didn't know what to do with myself, so I decided to catch a movie. And the only theater in town was showing *Jack*. The movie, starring Robin Williams, was about a baby born with a birth defect that causes him to grow at four times the normal rate. I almost left the theater, but something about it made me stay. I watched the parents agonize over Jack's safety, the ridicule of other kids. I saw this man-child, ten years old but looking forty, live life with all he had. His courage and strength and struggle and tears changed everyone around him.

I drove back to the Holiday Inn and got down beside my bed.

"This is all right," I prayed. "We can do this together. I accept whatever is ahead, knowing that it will be part of the great adventure. Thank you for letting me be angry; thank you for staying by my side."

Kneeling in a garden, weeping on your own,
longing for the play to change,
a rewrite for a tomb,
choosing in the darkness to play it to the end.
I come to you
who surely knows how hard it is to bend.
But bend I will into this wind
no matter how I ache
and trust that in the worst of times

you will not let me break.
I get up off this dusty floor and set my course
*   for home,*
safe in the truth: I'm not alone
because you faced your tomb.

Postscript: That evening Barry called me with the news that the test results had come back early, indicating "no problem."

Pushing Through the Night

You need to persevere so that when you have done
the will of God, you will receive what he has promised.
HEBREWS 10:36

I inherited my love of books and reading from my
mother, an avid reader. When I think of my childhood
home, there's always a book by Mom's chair. She taught
us to treat books with respect and care; after all, they
introduced us to other worlds and experiences.

Her bookshelves were lined with the works of Charles
Dickens (*David Copperfield* being the favorite) and great
works of the faith. And Mother loved the writings of A. J.
Cronin. Until the age of thirty-three, Cronin was a doctor
in London. Then due to poor health, he quit his practice
and moved to a quiet little village in Scotland. He decided
to try his hand as an author.

Like most worthwhile pursuits, writing was not easy.
Cronin quickly became discouraged, convinced that what
he had managed to commit to paper was worthless.
Surely he had been fooling himself to imagine that he
could write something of value. In despair he left his desk
and went for a walk. In the countryside he encountered
Angus, an old farmer patiently working the harsh peat. In
a *Reader's Digest* article he recalls that conversation, him
telling the old man that he was quitting as a writer.

The farmer listened and then said, "No doubt you're the one that's right and I'm the one that's wrong. But I've been working this bog all my days and never made a pasture of it. But pasture or no pasture I canna help but dig, for my father knew and I know that if you only dig for long enough a pasture can be made here."

That simple declaration of purpose was a turning point in Cronin's life. He went back to his desk and continued to work on the book that became *Hatter's Castle,* which sold more than three million copies and was translated into nineteen languages. The greatest victory here was that Cronin overcame himself and his self-doubt. As Shakespeare said, "Our doubts are traitors."

As a child of God, each of us has a divine call and destiny, and yet so often we are held back by fear and doubt. We are afraid of making a mistake, of looking foolish. We find it easy to believe that God can use someone else. But us? It requires a leap of faith to grasp hold of the truth that God can take us beyond our own abilities; we must simply trust him and keep pushing on through the night. The Word of God never says we mustn't make a mistake, but it has a lot to say about those who doubt. There's James 1:6, for example: "But when he asks, he must believe and not doubt, because he who doubts is like a wave of the sea, blown and tossed by the wind."

It is easy to believe that God can use our lives when we see immediate results, when positive feedback encourages us to push on. It is hard to keep walking when we see little sign that what we are doing is making a difference. I think of that farmer plowing away by the loch, knowing that what he was doing would one day make a difference. Perhaps he never saw it himself, perhaps his son or grandson finally gleaned the fruit of their labor—but a pasture was there.

Perhaps there is little immediate satisfaction in what you have been called to do, but if you will faithfully push on through the night the Lord is the one who carries a reward in his hands.

The earth seems dry and barren, Lord.
The wind is in my face.
I think of laying down these tools
to find a better place,
and yet there's something in this soil
*   that calls to me to stay*
and follow through, to follow you,
*   to walk until it's day.*
Amen.

A Humble Heart

Lord, if you are willing, you can make me clean.
MATTHEW 8:2

I didn't expect it to be so beautiful. When I think of Texas, I think of big cities, huge cattle ranches, and steaks the size of Omaha. This was different.

Barry and I had flown to San Antonio and picked up a rental car to drive to a small town called Kerrville. I had been invited by Pastor Del Way of Calvary Temple to sing a couple of songs in the Sunday morning service and give an evening concert. The closer we got to our destination the more picturesque the scenery became. Rolling hills and green fields stretched out before us for miles.

"I could live here," I said.

"Me too," Barry replied.

"We could have five dogs and two horses and chickens and maybe a goat or two," I suggested.

"You and one dog and one cat is more than enough for me!" he said with a grin.

We arrived at our hotel and unpacked. We slept like babies and woke refreshed the next morning. As I sat in the church service I was moved by the atmosphere of worship. Even the teenage boys were singing with all their hearts. *This is a special place,* I thought.

After my last song Del got up to speak. His message was simple and startling to me. Like so many of the most powerful truths in the world, the kernel was simple truth. His message was taken from Matthew's gospel, a story I have known since childhood, and yet I heard it that day as if the ink were not yet dry on the manuscript.

A man with leprosy came and knelt before him and said, "Lord, if you are willing, you can make me clean."

Jesus reached out his hand and touched the man. "I am willing," he said. "Be clean!" Immediately he was cured of his leprosy (Matt. 8:2–3).

Matthew says that multitudes were following Jesus wherever he went, but there was something different about this man, even apart from his leprosy. The Greek word used here for *knelt* is from the root "to worship," to kneel down and lick someone's hand like a dog, in total humility. I'm sure that there were many needs present in the crowd that day, but the one who received his miracle was the man who humbled himself and knelt at the feet of Christ and worshiped, saying, "If you are willing, you can make me clean."

In bed that night I thought about that for a long time. How can we appropriate the faith and humility of this man? So many of us go to great lengths to follow the "latest move" of God. We make sure we attend the right conventions and read all the right books; we are "with Christ," part of the "in" crowd. But I think God asks us simply to fall at his feet and worship, to acknowledge that we cannot heal ourselves, that we are dependent on him every moment. Going deeper in our lives with God is a more solitary life. I am committed to community. It is the church, it is our calling, but it is only as we are real with God and broken before him that we have anything to bring to one another.

I used to try and find a perfect formula to worship at home. I would get out a hymnbook and sing my way through many of the great hymns of the faith. Or I would work with a book of liturgy. I would sing worship choruses until my cat hid under the bed, but the formulas were barren to me until I began literally to prostrate myself on the floor before the Lord, confessing my weakness and sinfulness. Now as I meditate on the goodness of God, I find myself singing or weeping or laughing. Worshiping God.

I have no ten steps to offer you, but I do encourage you to follow the lead of a leper and fall at the feet of Jesus and worship him. We are called to be a home for God, a prepared room where he can live and pour out his life and love.

Falling at your feet I throw my life into your care.
I worship at your feet;
my heart has found a true home there.
Nothing in my hands I bring,
my life my only offering.
My heart in broken gladness sings
That Christ has met me here.

Committed to Worship

Worship the LORD with gladness;
come before him with joyful songs.
PSALM 100:2

[The word] *cells*, as the monks call their rooms,
has nothing to do with prison cells.
Cell comes from the Latin word *cella*, related to the word
coelum, heaven, the place where one enjoys God.
BASIL PENNINGTON, *A PLACE APART*

I have enjoyed the presence of God in all sorts of places. Whether walking over the green hills of Scotland or down by the ocean as the waves crash over my feet, there is something about the beauty of God's creation that welcomes praise and worship, calls it from my soul.

But what about the dark days? What about the days when you are cut off from anything of beauty? Perhaps no one understands that better than Pastor Ha. He now lives with his wife and two children just a few miles from where I used to live in southern California, but he used to be the pastor of the largest church in Saigon. During some very difficult days for the church, he was imprisoned for six years, including sixteen months in solitary confinement. The prison was a dank, miserable hole. How do you worship in a place like that? What is there in your surroundings that would remind you of the goodness of God? Pastor Ha is a very unusual man. He discovered that if he put his head down the toilet in his solitary cell, he could preach to the prisoners in the cells below; he sang hymns of praise to encourage them and bring some comfort into their darkness.

Can you imagine such a thing? I have such a strong image of this godly man down on his hands and knees with his head down a toilet bringing words of life to dying men as he worshiped God, his life a testimony to his love for and devotion to Christ. I hear him singing:

> *Great is Thy faithfulness, O God my Father,*
> *There is no shadow of turning with Thee;*
> *Thou changest not, Thy compassions, they fail not;*
> *As Thou hast been Thou forever wilt be.*
> *Great is Thy faithfulness! Great is Thy faithfulness!*
> *Morning by morning new mercies I see;*
> *All I have needed Thy hand hath provided—*
> *Great is Thy faithfulness, Lord, unto me.*
>
> THOMAS CHISHOLM

Worship is a call. It is not a pat on God's back for giving us a good day or an answer to a particular prayer. Perhaps you find yourself in circumstances that are less than inspirational. As you look around at your life, you are disappointed with what you see. I ask you for a moment to think about our brother locked away from his wife and family—in a miserable jail cell with his head down a toilet, worshiping God. Remember that we worship God not because he has strewn our lives with a Christmas list of gifts but because he is God; he is our God and he is worthy to be praised.

Great is Thy faithfulness! Great is Thy faithfulness!
Morning by morning new mercies I see;
All I have needed Thy hand hath provided—
Great is Thy faithfulness, Lord, unto me.

A Royal Invitation

> But you are a chosen people, a royal priesthood,
> a holy nation, a people belonging to God,
> that you may declare the praises of him who called
> you out of darkness into his wonderful light.
>
> 1 PETER 2:9

I started off by myself at nine o'clock in the morning. I figured I would break for lunch at twelve-thirty and keep going until the stores closed at five. What do you wear to meet a princess?

In two weeks I was to cohost a Royal Gala concert at the Royal Albert Hall in London for Save the Children Fund. Princess Anne was the patron of this charity and would be present in the royal box. My cohost and I would be presented to the princess at the end of the evening. I tried on dress after dress. Too stuffy. Too expensive. Too frilly. Too tight.

Eventually, as the sun was beginning to set, I found a dress I liked and flopped down in Harrod's tearoom for a much-needed cup of tea. I went over the instructions that my cohost, British rock star Alvin Stardust, and I had received from the palace. It was made very clear that there was a right way and a wrong way to address royalty. When the princess was first introduced to us, we were to refer to her as "Your Royal Highness." After that, we could call her "Ma'am." The previous evening, at home in front of my mirror, I had practiced curtsying, and the best I could do looked more like fainting than curtsying.

The evening was a huge success. The Royal Albert Hall is one of the most beautiful concert venues in Europe, and on that night it sparkled. The British Broadcasting Company televised the event. When the last encore was taken and the stage lights went down, it was time to be presented to the princess.

I stood in line beside Alvin and waited. Suddenly there was a commotion and the royal party approached. As I watched the elegant princess walk toward me, my mind went completely blank. *What do I call her?* I racked my brain, but I could not remember. *Is it "Your Majesty"? . . . No, that's the Queen . . . Is it . . . ?*

Suddenly I heard a man's voice. "This is one of tonight's presenters, Miss Sheila Walsh."

I looked at Princess Anne and said the only thing that came to my mind: "Hello!"

People have been beheaded for less!

She was very gracious, however. She smiled and shook my hand, telling me how much she had enjoyed the evening. As she moved along the line, Alvin Stardust glared at me as if I were a terrorist.

In Britain you are raised to hold the royal family in a place of great respect and honor. You never speak unless you are spoken to; you bow or curtsy when you are introduced; and when they move on, the conversation is over.

Earthly royalty should be honored and treated with respect but their rule is limited to this earth; their kingdom is not eternal. Our God is a majestic ruler who would only have to speak a word and every throne would crumble, every earthly power be diminished. It is so amazing then to think that we who trust in Christ have access through his blood to the very throne room of heaven itself. What a gift through the sacrifice of Christ.

I spent so much time getting ready for my "big day" in London, but so often I enter carelessly into the presence of the King of Kings. God is our Father, so we enter his presence with confidence through Christ. We don't have to prepare and remember the perfect greeting. Read the psalms and you can see that. But it's easy to forget that God is also the Lord of the universe. Let us enter with reverent worship.

> *Holy, Holy, Holy!*
> *Though the darkness hide thee,*
> *Though the eye of sinful man*
> *Thy glory may not see,*
> *Only thou art holy;*
> *There is none beside thee*
> *Perfect in power, in love, and purity.*
>
> REGINALD HEBER

Special Moments

Glorify the LORD with me; let us exalt his name together.
PSALM 34:3

I had one of those moments today. I was standing in the kitchen as the sun was setting behind the hills. Lights were beginning to dot the hillside, and the temperature was dropping to a comfortable place. Bentley was in the yard, lying peacefully by the flower beds, eating a bone, and I could hear Barry singing in the shower. I looked across the kitchen into the den and my eyes rested on the navy blue stroller we have purchased for our son. Since it has no human occupant at the moment, we have placed our old teddy bears inside.

I put the kettle on to boil water for tea. As I opened the refrigerator to get the milk, I stopped to look at the photographs that grace the door. There is one of Bentley as a puppy; he's looking a little lost and wears a big green ribbon round his neck. There is one of my mother and my aunt Mary, who, at eighty, still lives by herself in a village just outside my hometown. There is a picture of my brother, Stephen, holding his son who will be a year old when our boy is born. Stephen holds him with such tenderness; as I think back to playing football in the yard and climbing trees together, it hardly seems possible that my little brother is a daddy. Then my eyes turn to a picture of Billy and Ruth Graham at home in North Carolina, books scattered everywhere, reflecting Ruth's passion for reading. There is a picture of my family gathered together last Christmas, everyone wearing silly party hats at my insistence.

During this brief reverie I heard no traffic noise or dogs barking; it was as if for a moment all the world was at peace. Suddenly I felt as if my heart was overflowing with praise to God for his goodness to me. I was surrounded by all the things that remind me of the grace and mercy of the Lord. I felt the baby kick and went to join Bentley in the evening air.

I prayed, "Lord, there are no words that could even begin to thank you for all you have done for me. I feel as if I am the richest woman on the planet. I pray for this little one moving inside of me that he will grow up to know you intimately for himself. Please help Barry and me to love him and prepare him to stand on his own with you." The next moments of silence felt holy, as if all I could do was rest in the presence of the Lord.

We look for spiritual moments in places where we think they should occur, as we gather to worship or as we kneel in prayer, but sometimes we are gifted — when it seems as if the Lord graciously allows his glory to visit our kitchen. Let us savor those moments when no one else can see us and nothing intrudes into our vision but Christ alone. Savor the moment and rest in him.

So I say to you, as the psalmist said to me today:

Glorify the LORD *with me; let us exalt his name together. Amen.*

An Unutterable Beatitude

Come, let us bow down in worship,
let us kneel before the LORD our Maker.
PSALM 95:6

Barry faxed me a devotional thought from his desk calendar today. It comes from the writings of A. W. Tozer:

> When the Holy Spirit is permitted to exercise his
> full sway in a redeemed heart there will likely be
> voluble praise first; then, when the crescendo rises
> beyond the ability of studied speech to express,
> comes song. When song breaks down under the
> weight of glory, then comes silence where the
> soul, held in deep fascination, feels itself blessed
> by an unutterable beatitude.

I was introduced to the writings of A. W. Tozer by my former boss at British Youth for Christ, Clive Calver—a committed Tozerite. We traveled all over the United Kingdom giving church and citywide presentations on the power of prayer and the impact of worship on the life of a city. I was a worship leader and Clive would speak. We saw God move in some remarkable ways, as ordinary men and women forgot about their lives and worries for a while, caught up in waves of praise to the Lord. For me the most memorable nights were when a silence would fall on the worshipers. It was as if we could not move or say a word, because we were on holy ground.

It's not very difficult to lead rousing worship; people love to sing at the top of their lungs, particularly when there is a great crowd and all are committed to the same purpose. But silence before God is something else. It is as if you enter another room where words would be out of place and redundant.

I wonder if sometimes we gather for worship but leave too soon. We are encouraged by the volume of praise; it lifts our spirits, allowing us to lay aside our burdens for a while. But if we would wait, there is more. It is God's response to the worship of his children. An "unutterable beatitude" or blessing.

I watched one year as the Academy of Motion Pictures gave a special award to a veteran actor. Before he was invited to take the stage, we were treated to a brief overview of his prestigious career. Many of his industry colleagues praised his work. As he walked onto the stage the applause was deafening; he stood for a few moments enjoying the support of his community. Eventually the clapping subsided, but before he was able to make his speech the music played him off. *Sorry, time's up.* It was clear that he wanted to respond but the evening had moved on.

I think sometimes we do the same in our worship. We love to tell God how much we adore him, how he has changed our lives. We revel in the tidal waves of song, but then "time's up" and we move on. If we would just wait on God, let the silence fall, we could be gifted with the response of a loving Father to his children. In that holy moment we could receive a beatitude, a blessing that no human words could begin to frame.

A rising cloud of song, of music,
soars above the crowd,
lifted by the hearts and souls
    of those who gather now.
But just beyond the doors of singing
waiting for us all,
the Father's hands upon
    our heads would fall.
Amen.

Pure Joy

Though you have not seen him, you love him;
and even though you do not see him now, you believe in
him and are filled with an inexpressible and glorious joy.
1 PETER 1:8

This morning I had a long list of things to do. The house needed cleaning and our refrigerator was almost empty. I felt weighed down. I had been awake since four o'clock, wondering how we would take care of several things, turning them over and over in my mind and finding no immediate solution.

It used to be that when I felt that kind of anxiety grip my stomach, I would throw myself into everything, trying to make all the pieces fit. By the time my husband would come home from work, I would be as crazy as a starved pit bull.

Not anymore. Now I run away. "Okay, Bentley, we're out of here."

I pick up my golden retriever's leash and head for the car. His tail wags with wild abandon. I open the passenger door for him, and he jumps in. He takes his usual place sitting upright with his nose against the side window. As we get closer to the beach, I roll down his window so he can enjoy the fresh sea air and say hi to every passerby.

This being a weekday, I am able to find a parking spot close to the ocean. I take a deep breath of the salty air, cool for California. I stop to pick up a cup of coffee and fill B's bowl with water and then we head for the boardwalk. The surf is high and two young men in wet suits ride the waves with the passion of rodeo cowboys. I can see the outline of the island of Catalina like a cutout from a magazine pasted to the sky. An old man stops to talk to us: "Fine-looking dog you have!"

"Thanks," I reply. "His name is Bentley."

"Well, hi there, Wesley," he says.

Bentley licks his hand, prepared to let the name thing go.

"Used to have one of these myself," the man continues. "You get a lot of love from a dog. I had a cat first, but she was very stuck on herself."

I smile in agreement, thinking of my cat, Abigail, who is indeed very stuck on herself.

"Saw a poster one day," he continues. "Picture of a big ol' ginger cat saying, 'If you want a friend, buddy, buy a dog.' So I did!" He walks away, laughing at his own joke. I wrap him in a prayer as I watch him shuffle down the boardwalk.

A toddler points to Bentley, and his mother brings him over to pat the dog's head. I hold B's collar. He is still a puppy, but at sixty-two pounds his enthusiasm could bowl a boy over. "What a beautiful little boy," I say to the woman.

"Thank you. We think so too," she says with a warm smile. "We almost lost him when he was born. He is our little miracle." The little miracle sees a bird on the sand and is off for his next adventure.

I watch two children build a castle and think back to my childhood in Scotland. My brother, Stephen, and I used to build formidable forts and castles with intricate turrets and moats. I would decorate the walls with seashells, but of course our work of art was always gone the next morning. I would cry out in disappointment, seeing the little pile of shells alone on the sand. And then we would start all over again.

As I said, this morning I was running away. When life seems overwhelming, I've learned to take myself out of the situation, go to the ocean, and let God touch me. I don't take my list and pray over every item; I let God find me through old men and children and a waggy-tailed dog.

When I sit in despair at home, all I can see is myself and all the things that I need to do. When I weave myself into the tapestry of my town, I feel my selfish focus drift away. Sitting on the boardwalk, I think about the old man and wonder if he is alone. I make a mental note to look for him next time I am here. I think about that precious child gifted back to heartsick parents and pray that he will find his home in Christ at an early age. I consider the bird that evaded his sticky little hands; God knows its flight. I feel the companionship of Jesus. It's as if we are both smiling at the wonder and beauty of his work. I take a deep breath of the salty air. I know that my list still exists, but sitting here side by side with the Lord, I remember more important things. I remember his love, his grace, his timing.

Down on the sand the little boy runs to catch another bird and falls flat on his face. He is laughing, his mother is laughing, the bird is laughing, and so are my soul companion and I. I take another breath of the ocean spray. Joy is a gift.

In moments like these, as I watch the parade of life before my eyes, the emotion that sweeps over me goes far beyond happiness. It is pure joy.

When you welcome God's companionship in the darkest hours of your life, when you keep on walking by faith on the darker parts of the path, you are gifted with moments of wonderful elation—as if you are joining with heaven in a celebration that is a tiny shadow of what it will be like when we get home. The closer we push into the heart of God, the more we are swept away by the joy that is his breath and life and gift to us all.

Singing through the roaring ocean,
dancing on the crested waves,
all creation joins in telling
heaven's never-ending grace.
Sunshine spills across the water.
Seagulls rise on summer air.
Lord of Glory,
this your story
told to all who gather here.

A Grateful Heart

And he directed the people to sit down on the grass.
Taking the five loaves and the two fish and
looking up to heaven, he gave thanks and broke the loaves.
Then he gave them to the disciples,
and the disciples gave them to the people.

MATTHEW 14:19

"What a day!" said Peter.

"I can't believe how long this crowd has stayed," Andrew added.

"They need to go home now. They're hungry, and I don't know about you, Andrew, but I am starving, and I've had enough of a crowd for one day. I'm going to tell Jesus to send them home."

Peter made his way through the vast crowd. Babies were crying. Children were chasing each other, jumping over unsuspecting adults. A few people had decided to take a nap on the hillside.

"Master, the people are hungry," Peter began. "I think you need to send them home now. I've had a look at their faces; they're exhausted. They need to eat."

"Then feed them, Peter," Jesus said. "Don't send them away."

Peter felt that old exasperation rise to the surface. This was such an impractical suggestion.

"We have five small loaves and two fish. Little fish," he said. "All we have is a boy's lunch, and you want us to feed this crowd?"

"Bring the food to me," Jesus answered.

Peter went back to where Andrew and the others were standing. "Is he going to send them away?" Andrew asked.

"No, he's not," Peter replied. "He wants us to feed them with a packed lunch."

"What?" Thomas exclaimed. "That's ridiculous."

"Just take the bread and fish to him," John said.

They all made their way through the people until they stood at Jesus' side.

"Here it is," said Peter, holding up a small parcel.

Jesus looked at the men and then lifted the tiny offering to heaven and said, "Thank you."

That is so radical to me! Imagine yourself in this position. Thousands of people are hungry. They are looking to you to feed them, and all you have is a tuna sandwich. At best, I can see myself on my face before God, begging him to do something. Jesus doesn't do that. He doesn't ask God to do anything. He just says, "Thank you." To me that says that his complete and utter trust is in God. It would have made no difference if a fast-food restaurant had suddenly appeared on the hillside, Christ's trust was in God, not in what shape the miracle took.

How wonderful to live in and with such confident gratitude. Can you imagine what a relief it would be? I spend so much time worrying about how things are going to work out rather than just giving thanks.

Barry and I rent a home. Today we received a letter telling us that we have to vacate the house three weeks before the baby is due. I look again at the life of Christ and I lift my eyes to heaven and I say, "Thank you."

Maybe you have a need that seems overwhelming. Try trusting God for his provision. Try looking up and saying "Thank you."

> *Joyful, joyful we adore thee,*
> *God of glory, Lord of love!*
> *Hearts unfold like flowers before thee,*
> *Praising thee, their sun above.*
> *Melt the clouds of sin and sadness,*
> *Drive the dark of doubt away.*
> *Giver of immortal gladness,*
> *Fill us with the light of day.*
>
> HENRY VAN DYKE

Thank you, Lord, that you know our needs even before we speak a word. Help us to look to you with a grateful heart.
Amen.

Letting Go

Do not be anxious about anything,
but in everything, by prayer and petition, with thanksgiving,
present your requests to God. And the peace of God,
which transcends all understanding, will guard
your hearts and your minds in Christ Jesus.

PHILIPPIANS 4:6–7

What a promise! This is an all-inclusive verse. Do not worry about anything. Don't worry about the children or your car payment or your job or your health. Whatever is on your heart and mind, bring it to the Lord in prayer and in petition and do it with thanksgiving. Thanksgiving is such an important part of the process because it speaks to trust and confidence.

Imagine that my car was broken down by the side of the road and two cars pulled over to help. The first driver who offers to look at the engine says he has no experience with cars; he's quite unmechanical—makes doughnuts for a living—but he's willing to take a look. The second driver is a car mechanic. I would be grateful to the first driver for stopping, but I wouldn't have any confidence in his ability to fix the problem. I'd rather he go for coffee and doughnuts than look under the hood! With the second driver I wouldn't just be grateful that he stopped; I would also have confidence that he knew what he was doing and that the end result would be favorable.

When we take our prayer requests to God and then continue to worry, it is as if we are saying, "Thanks so much for stopping to listen to me, but I'm not sure you can help." In our souls we sense the dissonance in that line of thinking. We believe that God is able to do what he says he will do, why then is it so difficult to rest in this promise that Paul brings before the church in Philippi? *Don't be anxious about anything.*

I think our need for control interferes with our trust in God. Joy and control do not make good roommates. I struggle with this daily. I've always found it hard to delegate. I figure if I do something myself then I know it will be done and done the way I think it should be. This spills over into my relationship with Christ. *Doing* makes me *feel* as if progress is being made—though that isn't necessarily so.

I face a number of situations that lack closure. I see clearly that I have two choices. I can bring these things to God and then spend the rest of the day trying to work out how I can "make things happen." Or I can bring my requests before God's throne of grace with a prayer of thanksgiving and confidence in him and wait on the Lord. The real difference is what happens in me after my initial prayer. If I make the first choice I continue to worry and fret over the outcome. If I take the second way, the way by which Paul exhorts us to live, I come to an awesome promise: "The peace of God, which transcends all understanding, will guard your hearts and your minds in Christ Jesus."

What a gift! The Word of God could not be clearer here. If we will relinquish control of our lives and place our trust in God with absolute confidence, then the peace of God, which is beyond human understanding, will cover us, protecting our hearts and minds. This is true joy. Joy that G. K. Chesterton called "the giant secret of the Christian."

Lord Jesus,
Today I choose to let go.
Today I choose to trust you.
Today I bring my life to you with thanksgiving,
my heart to you in prayer.
My questions I leave there.
Today I choose to let go.
Amen.

Never Too Late

Rejoice in the Lord always. I will say it again: Rejoice!
PHILIPPIANS 4:4

I smiled when I read the poster in the window of the mall beauty salon: "It's never too late to be what you might have been." It was surrounded by pictures of the latest hairstyles and colors. I guess that was supposed to be the message: It's never too late to be a blond if that's what you know you are deep inside! The quote was attributed to George Eliot, author of the classic *Silas Marner*. I'm not sure that's how Eliot intended the quote to be used, but I think it's a wonderful statement and a spiritual truth. In God it's never too late to be what you might have been. So many people walk through life with regret. That seems like such a wasted, draining emotion to me. We are not powerless in our lives to make change, to start over again, to learn to do better next time.

I recently read a wonderful poem by Hugh Prather, from his book *Notes to Myself,* that captured this thought so beautifully:

> *If I had only forgotten future greatness*
> *and looked at the green things and the buildings*
> *and reached out to those around me*
> *and smelled the air*
> *and ignored the forms and the self-styled obligations*

*and heard the rain on the roof
and put my arms around my wife
and it's not too late.*

There is so much in life that is wonderful, and it's not too late to grab hold of it. It's not too late to be kind, it's not too late to be loving, it's not too late to tell the truth, to be honest. It's not too late to walk by the ocean, it's not too late to pray, it's not too late to tell your children that you love them, it's not too late to tell the Lord that you love him.

*It's not too late to be what you might have been.
I saw myself a prisoner to all the things I've been.
I saw the play repeat itself reliving every scene.
But then I heard a voice that said
step out and choose again,
step out and live, step out and love,
be what you might have been.
Thank you, Lord,
Amen.*

Come Home

What good is it for a man to gain the whole world,
and yet lose or forfeit his very self?
LUKE 9:25

One of my most treasured books is *Beside the Bony Brier Bush* by Ian Maclaren. I have an old copy first owned by a George Seull in 1898 and gifted to me by Ruth Graham. I love the stories told in true Scottish brogue — seven stories, all with a message of deep spiritual truth. As Ian walks the reader through the highlands, I can see the heather and the bright yellow gorse bushes and the fields of bluebells waving in the wind. But the story that I go back to over and over again is about Lachlan Campbell and his daughter, Flora.

Lachlan was a hard man, a devout believer who held the scales of justice tightly with little mercy or grace. One evening he brought a case of discipline before the church board. A young girl, he explained, had left home for the evils of London; she wasn't expected to be seen again. He came with a recommendation: that her name — the name of his own daughter, Flora — be struck off the church roll. The men in the fellowship were heartbroken for Lachlan. But they refused his recommendation; they would not take Flora's name off the roll, saying, "In the Lord there is mercy and with him is plenteous redemption."

Lachlan stood before them in silence, and the minister took the broken man to his house. He sat Lachlan by the fire and like a father asked him to explain what had happened. Lachlan pulled out a letter from Flora in which she poured out her heart, asking her father to forgive her for running away — but she could no longer live by his strict standards. "Perhaps," she said, "if my mother had lived she would have understood me. My greatest regret, Father, is that I will never see you again in this world or the next."

"That's not the letter of a bad girl," said the minister kindly. "Just a sad one."

Lachlan got up to leave. "You won't take her name off the church roll, but I've taken her name out of the family Bible."

For some time his neighbors in Drumtochty watched lonely, solitary Lachlan come and go until one woman could hold herself back no longer. Marget knocked on his door and told Lachlan that she had come in the name of the Lord to tell him that the family shame was his and not his daughter's. "Where would we be," she said, "if God had turned his back on us as you have on your own daughter?"

With those words God pierced this proud man's heart. Marget sat down with him and wrote to Flora, telling her to come home; her father was waiting for her with arms open wide. Every night as Lachlan went to bed he left a light burning in the window — in case it was the night that Flora came home.

And one night she did. It was dark as she made her way toward her father's house. She was so afraid. She knew her father and his iron principles well. Finally through the woods she saw the cottage; it was ablaze with light, and she understood. Running to the door, she was too overwhelmed to knock or speak, but her father knew she had come, because the dogs, who had never forgotten her or written her off, barked for joy. Lachlan opened the door. Though he had never kissed his daughter in all her twenty years, he gathered her in his arms and kissed her. That night they opened the family Bible together and wrote,

Flora Campbell, missed April 1873
Found September 1873.
"Her father fell on her neck and kissed her."

Perhaps as you read these words you see yourself in Flora. In leaving her father's home for the big city, she was turning away also from his faith. I talk to many people who have lost the way home. Perhaps raised by strict, unbending parents, they throw their own faith away as they reject a standard that they feel is crushing them. My question is always the same: "Did you find what you were looking for?"

Perhaps you see yourself in Lachlan Campbell. Refusing to bend or compromise, you have written someone off. You have said, "I have no daughter. I have no son." Where would we be if God had done that to us?

Would-be pilgrim or weary pilgrim: If you have lost your way and you have lost hope, come home. The Father is waiting for you. It doesn't matter where you have been. All that matters is where you are going. And for those who have hardened hearts against someone, those who march on toward heaven without ever looking back, I hold up the picture of a father standing at the window, never letting the light go out. I challenge you to reach out and to wait and pray and love — for today could be the day a child returns home.

Thank you, Lord, that you have never given up on me.
I set my feet and my heart toward home.
Amen.

Rude Awakening

Weeping may remain for a night,
but rejoicing comes in the morning.
PSALM 30:5

I have never been a morning person, so it was a rude awakening when baby Christian came along. I remember saying to my mom that I would need to buy a new alarm clock so I could wake up and feed the baby. She laughed. I didn't know then that babies come fully equipped with their own, not-to-be-ignored alarm.

As Christians, we all are morning people. We live now, as C. S. Lewis said, in the shadowlands, and we wait for morning.

I can think of many "shadowy" moments in my life. And I know, if we could see the joy of the morning, we would make it through those dark nights. I think about how differently I would have handled my dark time if Christ had handed me my baby boy and said, "Sheila, this is your son. He won't be born for a few more years. Now look at him. He needs you to find courage to get up and get emotionally well." How much easier it would have been to hold that precious life, look into those eyes, and find a reason to go on. But that didn't happen. Instead, Christ was there. And he asked me to get well and to believe, in faith, that he would make the crooked in my life straight.

So it was that Christian came into my life, bringing the joy of the morning to Barry and me. My delivery was easy compared to some horror stories I had heard, but it was quite enough for me. Barry and I had faithfully attended childbirth classes, and I had practiced breathing until I was hyperventilating. The nurse who had taught the class walked us through the various transition stages of labor and the breathing that would be appropriate for each stage. I have since decided she was actually a nightclub comedian in disguise because what she told us was a joke.

Christian wasn't due until the end of December, but at my checkup on December 12, pains hit me out of nowhere. Fortunately, my doctor's office was right next door to the hospital, and I was admitted immediately.

"What happened to the transitions?" I wailed to my husband. "I'll sue that nurse."

"Keep breathing, honey," Barry said lovingly. "You're doing great."

"Doing great! Are you kidding?" I replied. "Come over here and say that, and you'll be lucky if you ever breathe again!"

But Barry was too busy putting on a Christmas CD he thought would help me relax. I still have vivid memories of lying on a bed in the most excruciating pain I have ever experienced and hearing, "Just hear those sleigh bells jing-a-ling, ting-ting-ting-a-ling too."

At 5:20 A.M., December 13, Christian Walsh Pfaehler came bursting into the world at seven pounds, eight ounces. It's impossible to put into words the emotions that washed over me in great waves as I looked into the eyes of this little lamb we had prayed for for so long.

At 9:00 that evening the nurse sent Barry home and told me to get some sleep. She gave me a strong painkiller the doctor had prescribed, and I fell asleep almost immediately.

I woke up with a start. I looked at the clock and saw it was midnight. Where was I, and what was that funny noise beside me? I sat up too quickly, and my head spun. I looked to my left and located the funny noise. Apparently it was hungry. I wasn't sure what to do. I eased myself out of the bed, bent over the crib, and picked up my boy.

"I want to apologize if I don't get this right at first," I said as he stared up at me. "I'm a beginner, and I'm really not sure what I'm doing."

I took him into bed with me, and he nestled in.

"I'm kind of old to be a first-time mom, but I promise you I'll do my best."

He seemed oblivious to our first talk, but I carried on anyway. "But the best thing that we have going for us, little lamb, is that Jesus loves us both, and he'll help us." I looked down, but he was asleep, and in a few moments so was I.

Whatever you're going through at the moment, remember this is not the end of your story. We are morning people, called to live by faith and not by sight, to lift our hearts to God in the darkness because we have the promise of the morning.

Lord,
In the darkness be my light
In the silence be my song
In the stillness be my hope.
Amen.

Shaggy Friends

But when you give a banquet, invite the poor,
the crippled, the lame, the blind, and you will be blessed.
Although they cannot repay you,
you will be repaid at the resurrection of the righteous.
LUKE 14:13–14

We rang the doorbell, and the resulting sound of barking and scampering paws on hardwood floors was deafening. I laughed as I looked through the door's glass pane and saw four shaggy dogs running over each other in a desire to be first to the door.

The door opened, and Barry and I got down and greeted our shaggy friends before we even said hello to our hosts, Karalyn and Joe.

"What a menagerie!" Barry said as the smallest dog licked him over and over. We sat in our friends' study drinking iced tea, and eventually the dogs all found their places, flopping down exhausted from extending such an effusive welcome.

"Tell me about the dogs, Karalyn," I said. "You have quite a collection!"

"Well, Anabel came from an abusive home," Karalyn began. "I heard through a friend that this little dog was being beaten and left outside in the cold with nothing to eat, and I decided to do something about it. When we got her home, one of her legs had been broken in five places."

I looked at Anabel peacefully asleep on Joe's lap and found it hard to imagine that people could be so cruel.

"The little white one is having a hard time," Karalyn continued. "He's completely deaf and has a bad back and a sore paw."

Sunday, a hyperventilating Yorkie with a lilac bow in her hair, was getting on in years, and Jackson looked like he was growling till you saw his tail wagging fit to be propelled off his body. I have never seen dogs more loved or cared for than these four.

"Do you make a habit of rescuing dogs from the pound?" I asked.

"Yes, I do," Karalyn answered, smiling at her husband as he shook his head in wonder at his largehearted wife. "Everyone wants a perfect animal, a new one that looks great with no faults or limitations, but I've found the animals who have been all but tossed away have so much love to give."

Later I thought about what Karalyn had said and related it to people. So often we want to be with the "right" people, the crowd who looks and sounds like us. Yet Christ said, "Invite the poor, the crippled, the lame, and the blind, and you will be blessed."

I saw that in Karalyn. She is blessed by the love she receives from her tail-wagging friends and by knowing that she has made a difference in lives that needed a miracle.

Christ's story goes on to say that we shouldn't entertain those who can repay us but rather those who have nothing to give. In every church across America there are those who come lonely and leave lonely every Sunday. In each neighborhood, estranged ones live. Old people's homes are full of forgotten lives. No one comes to see these people anymore. I imagine these aged ones watch groups of friends and families talking and laughing together as they head out to eat or to a ball game. What a blessing it would be to them and to us if we really saw them and included them in our lives.

Lord, you saw me in my nakedness
    and loved me just the same.
You reached me in my sinfulness;
    I heard you call me friend.
So give me eyes to see, I pray,
    the ones who have no name.
Pour your oil on wounded hearts,
    Christ, on this earth again.
Amen.

Enjoy the View

May your father and mother be glad;
may she who gave you birth rejoice!
PROVERBS 23:25

I had no idea it would be this wonderful! Sure, I had
watched my sister as she cared for her sons and saw
her joy at every little step they took. But I had no idea
having my own child would be like landing over the rain-
bow and waking up in Oz.

I also had no idea my body could be stretched to those
proportions without bursting or that my heart could
either. I've noticed too that in the few moments of sleep
you get when your children are babies, God mysteriously
and wondrously tucks love into your heart. You find your
ocean of love is so deep it can carry you across the rough
water of sleeplessness. Billy Sunday said, "Mothers . . . fill
places so great that there isn't an angel in heaven who
wouldn't be glad to give a bushel of diamonds to come
down here and take their place."

But it's just for a moment. That's how it seems to me
already as I watch Christian sit up and crawl. There's a
whole world of growing and being and going ahead of
him, and if Barry and I do a good job, Christian will be a
strong, independent man. One day I'll watch him look
into the eyes of a young woman in a white dress, and his
eyes will be full of her.

But for tonight I get to tuck him into bed. I'll enjoy the scenery of his face, and I'll watch as his little lips move in his sleep. I'll enjoy how his hair curls at the bottom of his neck and tucks into his pajamas. And I'll sing to him a song of celebration I wrote when he was born.

Lay your tiny, golden head upon this pillow, dear.
There are angels watching over you
And the morning star is in the heavens close to you.
Can you see the moon is shining in your room
Tying silver ribbons in your hair?
May your sleep be sweet until the sun brings morning here.
And I never knew such a tender love
That could break my heart in two.
So I lay down gently now at Jesus' feet with you.
And I feel I'm lying on holy ground,
Such a gift God gave us in you.
So I kiss your velvet cheek and say a prayer for you.
Lay your tiny, golden head upon this pillow, dear.
There are angels watching over you.
And the morning star is in the heavens close to you.

Perhaps your children are all grown or you have no children. But look around you and see what you have. It may be a tail-waggin' dog who welcomes you home. Or a husband who notices you don't feel well and runs you a hot bath. Or a friend who calls at just the right moment. Whatever you see, stop for a moment and enjoy the view.

Lord Jesus,
Thank you for my life.
Thank you for those who make my life richer,
warmer, funnier, stronger.
Help me to stop and enjoy the scenery today.
Amen.

I Could Be a
Great Christian If ...

I do not understand what I do.
For what I want to do I do not do, but what I hate I do.
ROMANS 7:15

I could be so godly, if people didn't get in my face! It's dealing with all these humans that's doing me in.

This struggle came home powerfully to me when Barry, Christian, and I flew into Tulsa for a Women of Faith conference. We wanted to arrive Thursday afternoon or early evening, but the best flight time we could arrange put us into Tulsa after 10:00 P.M. Christian had been good during the trip, but we could tell, as we waited for our luggage at the airport, that he was very tired.

We had been told the hotel would send a courtesy van to pick us up because we had so much stuff, especially baby paraphernalia. But we saw no sign of the van once our bags finally showed up. Barry called the hotel in case they had forgotten about the arrangement. I could tell by his body language that he was becoming angry.

I knelt down beside the baby in his stroller. "This is when daddies like mommies to stay out of the way!" I said. "So we had better wait over here."

After fifteen minutes Barry came over to us. He was very upset. "The guy at the front desk said they were too busy, and we should catch a cab. When I told him we had too much stuff for a taxi, and we also had a six-month-old baby, he said, 'That's really not my problem' and hung up."

"How rude!" I said. "Oh well, let's take two cabs." We bundled into two cabs, and when we arrived at the hotel, Barry went inside to talk to the manager on duty. Christian and I decided to wait outside. After a little while, Barry hadn't reappeared so we went in to see what was happening. He was standing at the front desk arguing with two of the hotel staff. I overheard one of the insults directed at Barry, and something in me snapped. I marched over to the desk and told the red-faced employee that he was a jerk. We got our key and finally made it to our room.

Once the baby was settled for the night, I ran a bath. As I lay in the soothing water, I started a litany of all the reasons it was so hard to be a Christian — and all of those reasons boiled down to having to relate to people. Just as I was working my way into sputtering to God about how offensive people can be, I realized I was rationalizing my own behavior. I became overwhelmed by what I had said to those two hotel clerks.

I thought, *I'm here with the Women of Faith conference. I'm here to talk about God's love, and I just called the guy at the front desk a jerk. How can I possibly walk onstage tomorrow night?* I felt like such a hypocrite.

So I did the only thing I knew to do: I threw myself on God's mercy and asked him what I should do now. His response was as clear as a sunny day after a rain. God didn't speak to me in an audible voice, but I knew he was telling me to get out of the bath, dress, go downstairs, and ask for forgiveness. I dried off, pulled on jeans and a shirt, and headed for the door.

"Where are you going?" Barry asked, apparently worried I was ready for round two with the desk clerk.

"It's okay, honey," I said. "I'll be right back."

I dragged myself along the corridor to the elevator. It was now after midnight, we hadn't eaten for a long time, and I'd taken off all my makeup. I looked like I'd been in a train wreck. The doors opened in the lobby, and I walked toward the front desk. The two men were standing there with arms folded, watching me as I approached.

"I've come down to ask you to forgive me," I said. "What I said to you was so wrong, and I'm sorry."

They looked at me as if I had just confessed to shooting John Lennon.

Finally, one of them said, "I'm sorry too."

Well, that's all I needed to hear. I could have run up the fifteen flights of stairs (figuratively speaking, of course). I had headed down to the lobby with no joy and weighed down by my sin, but I returned to our room lighter than air because I was forgiven.

I don't tell you this story to suggest I'm proud of what happened. Far from it. I deeply regret when I dishonor God with my life, but I want you to know that none of us is alone in her struggles. When, like the apostle Paul, we do the thing we don't want to do, we are given an opportunity to put it right.

Are you having trouble living the Christian life because of people? Maybe, like me, you need to examine what responsibility you bear for the situation. What steps can you take to get right with God and to make amends to the people you have offended or hurt?

Lord Jesus, I make so many mistakes. Thank you that you forgive me and wash me clean. Thank you for loving me. Tell me how to right any wrongs I've committed. Amen.

Let Mama Out of the Trunk

Listen to your father, who gave you life,
and do not despise your mother when she is old.
PROVERBS 23:22

A friend of mine recently told me he now only talks to his mother by e-mail because it makes her more bearable. I asked him if he had ever discussed with her the difficulty they had communicating. He looked at me as if I had suggested he stick his hand in a blender. "You've got to be kidding," he said. "Talk to my mother? That's like trying to bargain with a scorpion!"

Since I've become a mother, I have a new appreciation for my own mom. When I realized what labor pains were all about, I wanted to buy her a small country! I now know, in such a deeper way, that the parent and the child are irrevocably part of the tapestry of each other's lives. How sad to try to ignore a part of that tapestry or "endure" its presence.

Why do we find it so hard at times to relate to our mothers, to speak the truth to those who gave us life? When I say "speak the truth," I mean loving, ongoing truth, not a stream of "I'm a jerk because you dropped me when I was two" accusations.

Part of the problem is we don't talk honestly to each other in our families. We feel guilty if we have negative feelings toward our parents. So we stuff those feelings and then wish we could stuff our parents! True love demands a different approach: honesty, taking risks with one another, and enduring some difficult moments because we want a real relationship.

One of the most freeing moments in my relationship with my mother was when I realized I wasn't responsible for her emotional well-being or happiness. I used to have an inflated sense of responsibility and wandered around for years like a demented nurse taking every family member's emotional temperature. But I quit my job. It was too exhausting, and I'm sure I was annoying.

In case you're stuck in that role with your family, especially with your mother, I offer this suggestion: Date your mother. Now, before you think I've taken a permanent dive off the wagon of sanity, let me explain. When you first began to date your husband or pursued a new relationship with a potential friend, you gave it all you had. You asked questions because you were hungry to know more about this person. You listened, and as trust and mutual respect grew, you shared your hopes and dreams with that person.

Our mothers had lives before we came along. But often we know very little about that young woman with hopes and dreams of her own who would lie awake at night and wonder how her life would turn out. Finding out who that woman is and was can be fascinating, just like discovering a new friend.

Often family members behave in set patterns simply because that's what we expect each other to do. It's a dance that has developed over the years between us. So take a fresh look. Put on a new record. Get to know your mother in ways you haven't before. Celebrate the woman she is. Say "Thank you." Send her flowers. Write her a note. Take her out to dinner. Buy her something she wanted as a child and never got. Take a good look. Move a little closer. And let Mama out of the trunk!

Dear Lord, today I want to thank you for my mother. Thank you for all the thankless moments she endured from me and went on loving anyway. Thank you for her time and patience and forgiveness. Help me to find new ways to express my love to her.
In your name and grace, amen.

Refuel Us Again

But Jesus often withdrew to lonely places and prayed.
LUKE 5:16

Quiet places can be found in the noisiest spots, if you have the ears to hear them. I discovered that with a cat in my lap, a bird on my head, and a rabbit at my feet.

I was in my first year of theology graduate studies, and one of the classes I chose was "Foundations for Spiritual Life." At the end of the semester, part of the grade depended on taking a silent retreat at a monastery. The idea of silence was intriguing. I thought back to my days at Heathfield Primary School and how often I had to stand in the corner for talking too much.

Brother Michael greeted us students the day of our retreat. He invited us to spend the day enjoying God's presence on the monastery grounds. We agreed to meet up again later in the chapel, but until then we had the day to ourselves. We all headed off in various directions.

I found a wonderful spot in the shade of an old tree. I sat for a few moments and enjoyed the scenery. It was a beautiful, clear day, and I could see for miles. I had a journal with me so I could write down whatever came to mind as I fellowshipped with God. I had my Bible and *Streams in the Desert,* my favorite devotional. I opened it to the reading for that day.

Halfway through the reading, a rabbit bounded across the path in front of me, and I stopped to watch its ears twitch as it sensed it wasn't alone. With a quick flip of its back legs it was gone.

I turned back to my book. In the distance I could hear a lone bird singing. Its whistle was plaintive and melodic. I listened for a while.

Then a large ginger cat parted a bush and walked across to where I was sitting with my back to the trunk of the tree. I scratched her ear, and she purred gratefully, settling down on my lap. I tried to read over her head, but she kept pushing the book out of the way to give me a better opportunity to scratch her ears.

This is no good, I thought. *I'm supposed to be meeting with God, not scratching a cat's ears. Sorry, Ginger, you're ruining the moment.*

I stood up and Ginger jumped to the ground, giving me a very disappointed look. She sauntered off. I walked a few paces deeper into the garden and came across a collection of gravestones. I knelt down to read the inscriptions and realized that each one spoke of a brother from the monastery who had died while serving there. The inscriptions were touching. These men obviously were loved and missed. I stood up and stretched and headed back to my tree.

I looked at my watch and saw that two hours had gone by, and I hadn't been very spiritual. I had all sorts of plans of what I would accomplish that day and definite expectations of what the day would look like, yet it wasn't working out that way.

You're a control freak, Sheila, I thought. *Let it go.*

I put down my books and journal and sat back against the tree. For the rest of the day, I just sat there. I didn't try to think holy thoughts or force my mind into a preconceived frame. I sat there with the rabbits and the birds and Ginger, who decided to give me a second chance.

It was a wonderful day. I found that as the sun began to set I had a deepened appreciation for the gift of solitude and for my sense of companionship with Christ as I sat surrounded by the wonder of his creation.

Holy moments come to us daily if we will ask for eyes to see. It may be the sun streaming through the window as you fold laundry. Or maybe it's lifting your friends to God while you vacuum. We can't always withdraw to quiet hillsides to pray, but Christ will meet with us in the quiet places of our hearts.

In the stillness I worship you, God of all glory.
In the quiet I sing to you, Lord of all life.
Amen.

Homecoming

If we confess our sins, he is faithful and just and will forgive
us our sins and purify us from all unrighteousness.

· 1 John 1:9

Ilove homecomings. That's one of the reasons I treasure every opportunity I have to take a trip back to my
native Scotland. On one such trip I was a guest singer at
a Billy Graham crusade. I sat with the rain bouncing off
the platform as George Beverly Shea sang the lovely
hymn,

> *Softly and tenderly Jesus is calling,*
> *calling for you and for me.*

I looked out at the crowd gathered in a Scottish soc-
cer stadium on that soggy Saturday afternoon and mar-
veled that Dr. Billy Graham could fill the place. If it had
been Chicago or New York, I would have expected a vast
sea of faces, but there, on my own home ground, I was
overwhelmed. I watched the crowd hanging on every
word.

> *Come home, come home*
> *All who are weary come home.*

Billy's message was simple and uncompromising. No
bells or whistles "wowed" the crowd, just a simple call was
made to "Come home." I looked out at shaved heads and

tattoos, children running through puddles, and wrinkled, weary old faces huddling under umbrellas, and I wondered what the response would be.

I wondered if the message sounded too good to be true. I wondered if it sounded too simple.

But then it began — like a waterfall, people began to stream to the front to receive Christ. I had to bury my face in my hands, overwhelmed with pure joy at being a spectator at such a homecoming. I thought of the Scripture, "I tell you that in the same way there will be more rejoicing in heaven over one sinner who repents than over ninety-nine righteous persons who do not need to repent" (Luke 15:7). I knew a big homecoming celebration was going on in heaven right then.

When the crusade was over, I was waiting at the side of the stage for my ride back to the hotel. A woman wrapped up in a plaid raincoat touched my arm. "I enjoyed hearing you sing tonight," she said.

"Thanks!" I replied. "Wasn't it a wonderful evening?"

"It was for me," she said. "I'll never be the same again."

"What do you mean?" I asked.

She stopped and looked at me for a moment as if struggling to put it into words. "I've gone to church all my life, but tonight, I came home."

I put my arms round her and hugged her, and the tears and the rain ran rivers down our faces.

I wonder if, like this woman, you've been circling the building for years but never have come home. It would be such a shame to sit in church every Sunday and listen to what's being said about God but never grasp that this is a personal invitation, a homecoming, a welcome mat thrown on the ground just for you.

"If we confess our sins, he is faithful and just and will forgive us our sins and purify us from all unrighteousness" (1 John 1:9). Isn't that great? Isn't that simple? All you have to do is pray.

Father, thank you that you love me. Thank you that Jesus died for me. I want to come home. Thank you for waiting for me. Amen.

Hair Today . . . Gone Tomorrow

Even to your old age and gray hairs I am he, I am he
who will sustain you. I have made you and
I will carry you; I will sustain you and I will rescue you.

ISAIAH 46:4

If God counts every hair that falls from our heads, he must be exhausted counting mine with all the abuse I ladle out to my head of hair. I think some women have an extra gene called the "hair coloring gene." We poor souls honestly believe we can buy a little box of color in a drugstore, and we will look like the woman pictured on the box. Never happens!

But that doesn't stop me. Oh, no! I march on down the road of hair destruction in search of that elusive perfect shade.

My first foray into this bleak and unforgiving world was with a shade called "warm coffee brown." *Sounds lovely,* I thought. *I like coffee . . . This will be good.*

It turned out black. Boot-polish black. Elvira black. A-crow-died-on-your-head black. *Never mind,* I consoled myself. *I'll try again.*

And so I did with "golden ash."

"How emotionally evocative," I mused. "I'll be like a tree in the fall, all shades of gold and amber."

Well, I was half right. I did look like a tree . . . in the middle of June. It was green, green, green.

I pressed on. Next I ordered what was described as "luxurious hair" by a woman on television with big hair. I thought, *I can't go wrong with this. I just attach these hairpieces under my own hair for full, flowing, glorious locks.*

When I opened the box the contents looked like a row of dead hamsters. I tried them on and had to admit I resembled a rather sad-looking cocker spaniel.

But the greatest damage I've ever done to my hair happened when I was eighteen years old and just about to leave my little Scottish town for a university in the big city of London. I was very excited and wanted to look hip. I had long, silky hair, which I decided was too old-fashioned. I needed a new look. So I bought a *Vogue* magazine and studied all the pictures. One model had hair that was cut in layers and softly permed. She looked beautiful.

"Do you like this hairstyle, Mom?" I asked one evening after dinner.

"It looks lovely, Sheila," she replied. "Why?"

"I'm thinking of having this done before I go to London."

She begged me not to. She begged me to wait and have it done in a London salon. But I wanted to arrive as the new me. I took the magazine picture to a small salon in my hometown of Ayr and asked one of the stylists if she could do it.

"Oh, sure, lassie. It'll be lovely!"

I decided not to look until she was finished. I wanted a big surprise. I got one. At first I thought something was wrong with the mirror, but then I realized I was looking at my head. I can't adequately depict the fright that was me. My hair was layered different lengths on each side. It was also fried. I looked as if I'd stuck my wet finger in an electric socket. I numbly paid and began to walk down the road.

I talked to myself as I went. "It's not as bad as you think. It'll be better when it's washed. Christ may return today."

Just at that moment I spotted my mom and my brother, who were waiting for me outside a coffee shop. Stephen was laughing so hard he was clinging to a pole to try to hold himself up. My poor mother was attempting to make him stand up and behave, but her efforts just caused him to laugh harder. He ended up lying on the sidewalk.

I was eighteen then. I'm forty-two now, and thankfully I've learned how to handle my hair. One other thing I've learned is that my worth to God has nothing to do with how I look or feel. He is committed to me on my good hair days and on my bad hair days. And when I make a fright of my spiritual life—even committing errors that seem "permanent"—Jesus can wash them away. He is eager to do so and will never laugh, regardless of how ridiculous I look.

If today, as you look in the mirror, you wonder if this is a face only a mother could love, remember, it's a face a *Father* loves!

Thank you, Father, for loving me through all my fragile, silly days. Thank you for holding me close to your heart, under your wing. Amen.

I Think I Can,
I Think I Can

Therefore, I urge you, brothers, in view of God's mercy,
to offer your bodies as living sacrifices, holy and pleasing
to God—this is your spiritual act of worship.
Do not conform any longer to the pattern of this world,
but be transformed by the renewing of your mind.
Then you will be able to test and approve what God's
will is—his good, pleasing and perfect will.
ROMANS 12:1–2

Nothing is worse than trying to squeeze yourself into something that doesn't fit. Just ask my friend Marlene! She was one of my bridesmaids and had to go through that awful ritual of being inflicted with a bridesmaid's dress. Because it was a winter wedding, I chose hunter green velvet dresses. Nancy, my matron of honor, lived in England so I had to guess her size and send it over hoping for the best. My other two bridesmaids were being fitted in Charleston so they were taken care of, but Marlene was another matter.

She was so busy she didn't have time to be measured for the dress but was fairly confident that she would wear a certain size. (Size withheld out of desire for continued friendship.) I told her the assistant in the store said a person should order a size larger than normal since bridesmaid dresses are usually cut small. But Marlene said no. I decided to order the larger size anyway and cut off the label. This seemed like a brain wave until it arrived, and Marlene asked me why I'd cut off the label.

"You ordered the bigger size, didn't you?" she said.

"I cannot lie," I replied. "Just try it on."

She came out of her bedroom in a few moments with a stunned look on her face. "It's too small!" she cried. "I can't zip it up."

We didn't have time to order a new one. We were stuck.

"Well, you just can't ever eat again; that's all," I said.

"Don't worry," she replied. "I have a plan." When Marlene said she had a plan, you can never tell what might happen.

The big day arrived. All the bridesmaids were dressing in my room, and sure enough, Marlene slipped into her attire and looked beautiful.

"How did you do it?" I whispered.

"I'll tell you later," she said.

Finally, we had a few moments together at the reception. "You have to let me in on your secret," I said.

"I was wrapped," she replied.

"You were what?" I asked.

"Wrapped like a turkey at Thanksgiving," she said proudly. "I went to a beauty salon every day and was trussed like a bird for the oven to melt me into the svelte figure before you."

We still laugh about that when we get together. I'm touched by the lengths my friend went to for my wedding day, above and beyond the call of duty. I know that what she went through was uncomfortable and unnatural.

But I wonder how often we do that to our souls as we try to fit into this world. The mold that this world would like to squeeze us into is an ill-fitting one. Instead, Christ calls us to be transformed in how we think, and to evaluate the messages that are sent to us every day through the television screen, on the billboards, and in the mall. We don't have to pull our hearts and souls in to accommodate this ill-fitting outfit that our culture would have us wear. Instead, we are free to be just us, renewed hearts and all.

Lord Jesus, thank you for setting me free from the tight clothes of this world to be dressed in your righteousness instead. Amen.

My Boat Is Sinking

Our mouths were filled with laughter, our tongues
with songs of joy. Then it was said among the nations,
"The LORD has done great things for them."
PSALM 126:2

Laughter will get you through many a tough situation
that otherwise would sink your ship. For my husband,
Barry, and me, our dream boat sprung a leak when we
were still at the airport. The writing was on the wall in
letters sixteen feet high, but we had on our holiday
shades, and nothing was going to dampen our spirits. We
were off to the love boat! Well, not quite.

Sandi Patty, Max Lucado, Susan Ashton, and I were
hosting a cruise from Boston to Bermuda. Barry and I
were so excited. We had never taken a honeymoon, and
this was going to be it. We were to be met at the airport
by a limousine and taken to the dock. During my
growing-up years in Scotland, we didn't even own a car.
Now thoughts of all those years standing at bus stops
were overprinted with images of being picked up in a big,
fat, shiny limo. Bliss!

No one was at the gate to greet us; so we assumed the
driver would be waiting at baggage claim. "They won't
want us to carry our bags," I said to Barry.

We reached baggage claim and scoured the scene for
a sharply dressed, uniformed man holding a sign saying,

"Barry and Sheila, your carriage awaits." Twenty minutes later the baggage area was deserted except for Barry and me and our luggage.

"What do you think could have happened?" I asked my equally bewildered husband.

"Stay here, and I'll call the cruise line," he said.

Ten minutes later he returned to report that they had forgotten about us and had suggested to him we should take a cab.

"I wish I had my camera handy," I said. "I'd love to snap a picture of us standing here in this deserted building. All dressed up and nowhere to go!"

We found a cab and were soon on our way to the dock.

"Which cruise line are you on?" the cab driver asked. We told him, but his only response was to say, "Ohh." I was beginning to suspect our love boat had started taking on major amounts of water.

The driver pulled up beside a lovely looking ship, and our spirits picked up.

"This looks great!" I said to Barry. "But why are all those people getting off the boat?"

"That's the crew," the driver said. "Two-thirds of them resigned this morning."

We climbed out of the cab and asked a man in uniform where we should put our bags to be taken on board. "If you ever want to see them again, I recommend you carry them yourselves," he replied.

I still have vivid memories of our struggling up the gangplank dragging our cases. When we reached the top, looking like refugees from a storm, one of the few people from the ship who hadn't resigned took our picture with a parrot.

Then we saw our cabin. I had imagined a lovely, spacious room with a view of the crystal clear waters below, fresh flowers in a vase, and music playing gently in the background. But when we opened the door, we both just stood there for a moment, stunned.

Then I lost it. I laughed so hard I fell over our bags. I wouldn't say the room was small, but we needed to take off our coats to get in. My pantry at home is bigger. We both laughed till tears ran down our cheeks.

"Let's go up on deck and get something to eat," Barry said. "You know what they say about all the great food on a cruise!"

When we arrived on deck, freezing rain greeted us, as did a line going all the way around the ship. "What's the line for?" I asked the person who had just joined it.

"Lunch," he grunted.

We were in that line for two hours and five minutes. All that was left of the lunch staff was one poor man who served cold pizza to twelve hundred people.

"Never mind," Barry said, as we both tried to squeeze into our cabin later. "We sail for Bermuda in ten minutes."

"This is your captain speaking," the voice over the intercom said. "I have some bad news. There is a hurricane at sea so we can't leave Boston harbor. Have a nice day."

You have to laugh! Laughter is a gift that will get you through the worst of times. Each of us can choose to lose it when life doesn't live up to our expectations, or we can let it go and laugh at the funny side of it all. Perhaps those who watch our jovial spirits will say, "Their God must be good."

Lord, thank you for laughter. Help me to see the hilarity of it all and to share it today. Amen.

Is Anyone Awake?

Behold, I am coming soon! My reward is with me,
and I will give to everyone according to what he has done.
REVELATION 22:12

Well, I'm glad that God's awake!" my sister, Frances, said as I finished telling her about the tornadoes that touched down in Nashville the previous weekend and which had blown themselves into my life but left me unscathed.

"Now let me tell you about my weekend," Frances said.

With the receiver cradled against my ear, I put on the teakettle as I listened. I just knew that this was going to be a good story.

"I volunteered through the church to sing at the local nursing home this past Sunday," she began. "I knew it wasn't exactly Carnegie Hall, but I wanted to bring a little joy to the senior residents who don't get out much."

"How many were there?" I asked innocently.

"Physically there or mentally there?" she replied with a smile in her voice.

"Just count the warm bodies," I said.

"Well, six people showed up. Three ladies fell asleep before I started. Another was off in a corner dancing to a tune that was different from the one I was singing, but the loudest one of all sat right up front, just under my nose. She was so close to me every time she sneezed I got a bath. Her hearing aid was turned up too high, and it was giving off high-pitched whining noises that would have driven a dog mad. One of the nurses tried to get her to back off a little, but the woman just yelled at the nurse and told her to shut up."

"Well, at least you had one enthusiastic listener," I suggested lamely.

"Not quite," Frances replied. "Every time I began another song she cried out at the top of her lungs, 'Oh, no, she's going to sing again!'"

We laughed for a while thinking about Frances's less-than-captivated audience.

"But, you know, Frances," I said, "what you said is right. God was awake. He didn't miss a single note."

Easy for me to say? Perhaps. But it's still true.

Do you ever feel as if you are killing yourself serving your children and your husband or your church or your friends, but no one seems to notice or appreciate you? We are told in so many ways what success looks like, what the woman of the nineties can do. Even in our churches we see those with high-profile ministries as the ones God is using.

I believe we need to resist that type of thinking. It's so discouraging—and it's so untrue. God sees our hearts, and that's all he cares about. He doesn't miss a single moment of a life lived out for him, whether it's in a spotlight or in a nursing home. That's why Frances will be back next Sunday being showered afresh by Bertha in the front row. Frances understands that even if Martha, Millie, and Mary are fast asleep, God is awake.

If everyone in your audience has dozed off or danced off to another tune, you might want to check again. There, in the corner, is God, watching and listening and appreciating you.

Lord, thank you for my life. Thank you that every day is a gift from you. Thank you that I can offer every moment to you, and you gather them all up. Today I give you all the great and small moments, and I live them for you. In Jesus' name. Amen.

Are You Finished with That?

Do not be anxious about anything, but in everything,
by prayer and petition, with thanksgiving,
present your requests to God.

PHILIPPIANS 4:6

Do you experience times when there doesn't seem to be enough to go around? Bills are piling up faster than paychecks, and anxiety is creeping into your mind.

Many such moments have occurred for me, making me acutely aware that the bread on my plate came from the Lord because my cupboard was bare. When I was part of British Youth for Christ, I was paid a minimal salary. Usually I had just enough to keep me in hose and shampoo—and on my knees.

One of my memories from that time is of Phil, a staff evangelist, and his wife who splurged one night and went to a nice restaurant for a steak dinner. While they were enjoying a lovely meal, Phil noticed that the man seated opposite them was leaving after only picking at the T-bone steak.

"More than three-quarters of that steak is left," Phil said to his wife indignantly. "What a waste!"

"Never mind what he's doing," she replied. "Enjoy your meal."

"But that's a huge piece of steak, and it'll go to waste," Phil continued. "They'll throw it out."

A few minutes passed, and then he said, "I'm sorry, but I just can't allow that to happen."

As he stood up, his wife hissed at him, "Sit down! What are you going to do?"

"Never you mind," he whispered. With that he sneaked over to the table, wrapped the large piece of meat in his napkin, and then slipped back into his seat.

"What did you do that for?" she asked in disbelief. "What are you going to do with it?"

"I'll give it to the dog," he said.

Two minutes later, the man who had been sitting at the table returned from the rest room to an empty plate. He called the waiter over and demanded to know what had happened to his meal. The poor waiter didn't have a clue as to its whereabouts, but he did casually wonder why that nice young couple was leaving without finishing their meal.

God's provision is seldom on the plate at another table. When you find yourself looking at a bank balance that couldn't keep a goldfish afloat, remember who you are. Your Father knows every need before you even voice it. He knows every unexpected turn of events. We are told by Paul to be anxious about nothing. "Nothing" is a pretty conclusive word. No thing, no part, no portion.

Whatever is weighing you down, stop what you're doing (which I guess at the moment is reading!), and with thanksgiving on your lips, bring your requests to God. You won't have to eat what's on someone else's plate; God will give you your own.

Thank you, Lord, that you care for me. Thank you that you see every need before I even voice it. Right now, with a grateful heart, I bring my concerns to you. Amen.

Help, Lord, There's a Cat on My Face

I lift up my eyes to the hills—where does my help come
from? My help comes from the LORD, the Maker of heaven
and earth. He will not let your foot slip—he who watches
over you will not slumber; indeed, he who watches over
Israel will neither slumber nor sleep.

PSALM 121:1–4

With all my years of traveling, I've slept in some
strange places. My great comfort when I'm far away
from home is that the Lord never sleeps but watches over
me whether I'm in Bangkok, Britain, or Boise, Idaho.

Some of the most powerful memories are from my
time as a youth evangelist in Europe. In Britain, an evangelist or singer would never stay in a hotel after an
evening meeting. Hospitality—and I use that word advis-
edly—would be extended from a member of the local
church. That hospitality is what drove me to lift my eyes
to my sleepless God to extend his help.

I remember staying with an old lady in Bristol, England, who had forty-three cats. I like cats, but forty-three
are about forty-two cats too many for me. I drank my cup
of cocoa with cat fur in it, and then thanked my hostess
and headed to bed.

"My little darlings will follow you!" she sang out after me.

I turned to see a plague of fur flow after me. "That's all right," I said. "I can find my room."

"It's where my darlings sleep too!" She smiled as she delivered this good news.

Fluffy, Muffy, and the gang made themselves comfortable on the bed, in my suitcase, and in my toilet bag. We were a family.

As I went to sleep I prayed, "Lord, please keep these beasts off me while I'm sleeping."

I woke up to find I was suffocating. I must be in a cave, a tunnel, I was drowning . . . no, it was worse than that. "Help, Lord, there's a cat on my face!"

Another town, another trauma. The couple who took me home after church seemed very nice and almost normal. As we pulled into the driveway of their home, I listened, but not a bark or a purr could be heard. Peace!

After supper the lady asked me if I minded sleeping in the garage. I said that was fine, assuming they had converted it into some sort of bedroom. But the man of the house pulled his car out of the garage and unfolded a camp bed in its place. It was November in England and very cold. I put on more clothes to go to bed than I had on during the day. (Where are forty-three cats when you need them?) Every thirty minutes the freezer would start up and *chug, chug* till I longed for a cat to put in each ear.

In the morning, as I lay there stiff from cold and discomfort, the husband started his car to go to work, and all the exhaust came flooding in. I thought, *I bet they're closet atheists, and they're trying to kill me!*

I stayed with a family in Holland for a week. They spoke no English, and I spoke no Dutch. The family shouted at me the whole time, apparently thinking it would make it easier for me to understand them.

I have lots of fun stories to tell and laugh about in the comfort of my own home. But every story is held together by the common thread of God's faithfulness through it all. He was my constant companion.

Is it ever hard for you to close your eyes at night? Do you worry about what tomorrow will hold or if you will be safe until morning? Psalm 121 makes it clear God never closes his eyes. He is always watching over you—even if you have fur in your mouth.

Lord, thank you that you are with me as I lay down to sleep. Thank you that I am never alone, for you are with me through the darkest night. In Jesus' name, amen.

Have I Got News for You!

Salvation is a gift and you can't boast about a gift.
You can only be thankful.

D. JAMES KENNEDY

It had been a long day for Grace. She finished her shift at the dollar store at five o'clock and hurried home to fix a meal for her husband, Stan, and their four boys. *What can we have that's quick?* she thought, as she stood in line waiting for the number ten bus. Her back ached from being on her feet all day, and the thought of going out again at 11:30 that night sent a throb deeper into her weary bones. Since Stan's accident the previous year, she had become the sole breadwinner and taken on job number two: cleaning at the local hospital three nights a week.

Grace arrived for her shift at one minute before midnight to join her two coworkers as they filled up their buckets with steaming hot water and shuffled down the corridor to begin the long night's scrub-down. All three women had a lot on their minds. Mary was worried about her daughter's grades. Stella hoped that no one noticed how often she slipped into the rest room to take a quick swig from the flask in her pocket.

Suddenly their private thoughts were punctuated by a noise down the corridor. They knew that no one should be in that area at that time of night. Grace, Mary, and Stella picked up their mops—poor weapons against any real threat — and stealthily approached the door from where the mysterious noise seemed to be coming. Warily, Grace opened the door . . . and beheld the most beautiful sight she had ever seen in her long, hard life. Filling the room with the wingspan of a thousand eagles stood an angel, a messenger from God, with this outrageous message:

> Grace! Have I got news for you! God is here! To you, Grace, with your varicose veins, your PMS, your two-pack-a-day habit . . . to you is born a Savior. Today. The love of God has come to you, Stella, and to you, Mary. God is with you.

This fable illustrates the simple, joyful message of the Gospel — just as it was presented on the first Christmas. After four hundred years of silence following the close of the Old Testament, God showed up on the night shift, to the shepherds. In the voice of his archangel he proclaimed salvation to the boys on the hill.

This radical gift of grace shows us that God's love is based on nothing we have done, but on who he is. Do you think God looked down at a few shepherds under the stars and thought, "These are the only guys who have their act together. I think I'll break the news to them first." I don't think so. God so longed for us to get the message of grace that he chose to display his glory to people like you and me who try so hard and fail so often. He shows up to people who slip into the bathroom for a quick shot of something to deaden the pain of life. He shows up to all the broken, lonely people of the world with the Good News: God is here!

It's hard to grasp that truth, living in this culture of ours where we worship at the altar of apparent success. We think that God will show up for the Billy Grahams, the Joyce Meyerses, the Women of Faith of this world—but not for us. It's as if we think that certain people have a hot line to heaven, a special number that God answers before he bothers with the regular office line.

It's time to go back to the Word of God and ask for eyes to see and ears to hear the way things really are. Christ came to the factory workers of his day. He was born on the wrong side of the tracks. He chose a fourteen-year-old virgin to be his mother. He was a blue-collar worker—he did manual labor all his adult life. His friends were a mixed bunch, and he was criticized for that. But grace won the day.

> While Jesus was having dinner at Matthew's house, many tax collectors and "sinners" came and ate with him and his disciples. When the Pharisees saw this, they asked his disciples, "Why does your teacher eat with tax collectors and 'sinners'?" On hearing this, Jesus said, "It is not the healthy who need a doctor, but the sick. But go and learn what this means: 'I desire mercy, not sacrifice.' For I have not come to call the righteous, but sinners."
>
> MATTHEW 9:10–13

That's the gift! The gift of grace is given to those of us who think we are worthy—until Christ in his mercy shows us we are not. The gift of grace is given to those of us who know we are not worthy—and yet Christ meets us in dark places, in hospital corridors, with cigarettes hanging out of our mouths and fear on our faces. He came to Grace, to Mary, to Stella ... to you and to me. What a gift! All we can do is kneel down and worship—and be thankful.

For it is by grace you have been saved, through faith—and this not from yourselves, it is the gift of God.

On the Road Again

 If and when a horror turns up you will then be given Grace
to help you. I don't think one is usually given it in advance.

C. S. LEWIS

When my son, Christian, was born, Barry's parents, Eleanor and William Pfaehler, were so far over the moon you could only see them on a very clear night. My husband is their only child. For twelve years they had prayed and waited for a baby. When Barry finally arrived, he was welcomed like rain on a parched desert. So when Eleanor's "baby" had a baby, the joy was almost more than she could contain.

Eleanor never imagined that she would live to see that day. Before Barry and I were married she had three heart attacks and was not expected to survive. But she did. "How I prayed that God would spare me to see my only child married and happy," she would often tell me when they came to visit us in our first home. Then at forty I became pregnant! I think she upped her tithe to fifty percent! What a joy it was to place that darling little boy, her only grandbaby, into her arms and see the look of wonder and fulfillment on her face.

I began traveling with Women of Faith when Christian was six weeks old. Before my first trip Eleanor asked, "What are you going to do with the baby when you're onstage?"

"One of the local churches is providing a baby-sitter," I explained. Eleanor didn't sound too thrilled, but Christian and I set off anyway.

When the pastor's wife ushered a young girl into my dressing room and introduced her as the baby-sitter, I was stunned. Rooted to the spot. The girl looked to be about five years old, with purple fingernails the length of California. She was chewing enough gum to pull out every tooth in my head. I paid her and sent her home.

"This is not going to work," I said to Barry on the phone, tears streaming down my face. "I can't leave him with a total stranger who looks like she's been out of diapers for four weeks."

That's when Eleanor stepped in. "We'll come," she said.

"To every conference?" I asked.

"Yes, to every one."

Now, I have been an international traveler for years. It's amusing to my family in Scotland that the ten-year-old girl who couldn't ride for more than two miles in a car without throwing up grew into someone who now has more frequent-flyer miles than the Archangel Gabriel!

For three years I traveled across Europe with Youth for Christ. I have flown to Hong Kong, Indonesia, Singapore, and Malaysia with Youth With A Mission. At one point I had more than half a million frequent-flyer miles on United Airlines. I'm sure I was in line for a free jumbo jet. I've taken bands on the road, new books or CDs on the road, purchased new outfits for the road. But it's quite another thing to take cancer on the road. That's what my mother-in-law did during the last two years of her life. Anytime Christian wasn't with me or Barry, he was with his nana and papa.

Perhaps you're thinking that every grandmother would love to see that much of her grandchildren. I'm sure that's true, but not every nana has liver cancer. I know that there were many weekends when Eleanor did not feel like getting on a plane and heading hundreds of miles away from home, but I watched as she refused to stay in bed and embraced grace for every difficult step. She could have sat at home in greater comfort, close to her own doctors if she needed them, but she chose instead to step out in faith. She gave sacrificially to all of us, and in doing so, she told me, experienced more of the grace and provision of God than she had known in her life before.

That's the mystery of the gift of grace. It shows up just when you need it. Not a moment too soon, but not a moment too late. We can live our lives nailed to a spot by fear, or we can reach out beyond ourselves and find a well of grace springing up just where we need it most.

I'm sure Eleanor had read the psalmist's words many times before, but when she took cancer on the road she *knew:* "The salvation of the righteous comes from the LORD; he is their stronghold in time of trouble" (Ps. 37:39).

God is our refuge and strength, an ever-present help in trouble. Therefore we will not fear, though the earth give way and the mountains fall into the heart of the sea, though its waters roar and foam and the mountains quake with their surging.

PSALM 46:1–3

Say "Thank You"

Were there no God we would be in this glorious world
with grateful hearts and no one to thank.
CHRISTINA ROSSETTI

I'm learning to stop for thankful moments. It's become a daily discipline of mine since I found that I was getting overwhelmed by all the daily stuff that "has to get done." Some of the feelings and fears I had before I was hospitalized for clinical depression were niggling at me again, buzzing around me like persistent houseflies. I've learned enough about what makes me tick to pay attention when I feel myself sinking. So I'm learning to stop intentionally throughout every day and lift my heart and soul to heaven and say, "Thank you!"

Giving thanks does wonders for my soul. It refocuses me on what's really important so that instead of dwelling on the fact that Christian just tried to flush my new pale blue suede pumps down the toilet, I can celebrate the gift of a child when so many arms are empty. Marcus Aurelius, a first-century Roman emperor, wrote that the most important thing a man can choose is how he thinks. We can dwell every day on the things that are not working and let them drag us down, or we can thank God for the simple gifts of grace he gives us every day if we have a heart to see them.

When Barry's mom's liver cancer had spread to the degree that she was receiving in-home hospice care, she told me about the many people who dropped by every day to say "hi" or to bring some crab soup to try to tempt her to eat. "Sometimes you don't stop to think how many good friends you have until a time like this," Eleanor said.

That thought sat on my shoulder like a small bird waiting to be fed. One March evening when we were visiting Eleanor in Charleston, Barry and I went out for a drive through the beautiful countryside. Suddenly the idea occurred to me: "Here's what I'd like to do," I said. "We'll have a good photo taken of you and Christian and me and get it enlarged, then cut it into pieces."

Barry looked at me as if the strain of his mom's illness had pushed me off a mental bridge. "Like a jigsaw puzzle," I explained. "We'll send a piece of the puzzle to each of our dear friends with a letter telling them why we're grateful to them, what they add to our lives, and how God has used them to fill in the missing pieces in our hearts. Then at Christmastime we'll invite them to a party at our house. We'll ask them to bring their piece, and we'll give them a gift specially chosen to highlight what they mean to us."

Barry was still looking at me as if I needed more sleep. I pressed on as we women have to when they don't get it.

"At the end of the evening we'll glue all the pieces back together, a visual picture of how our friends have added to our lives and how truly grateful we are for each one of them."

"What made you think of that?" Barry asked as we drove across the river.

"Don't you think it's a good idea?" I asked him.

"Sure I do," he replied, "but what made you think of it?"

"I don't really know. Sometimes I just want to find more ways to say 'Thank you.'"

"So you just thought of that?" Barry pressed.

"Yes!"

"And you're feeling all right?"

"Yes!"

I smiled. "It's like what we're trying to teach Christian. We tell him it's not enough just to say 'Sorry' when he does something wrong. Instead we ask him to tell us what he's sorry for. So perhaps it's not always enough to say 'Thanks,' either. We need to say what we're thankful for."

As I lay in bed that night after swallowing the two aspirin Barry gave me, I thought about how the same principle applies to our relationship with God. Instead of just tossing off a "Hey, thanks!" now and then as we hustle through life, why not make it a practice to thank him very specifically for his goodness to us?

In her book *Basket of Blessings: 31 Days to a More Grateful Heart,* Karen O'Connor shares her experience with just such a practice. "If you want to be content, to experience peace," a friend had told Karen, "write down your blessings — the things you're grateful for — on slips of paper and put them in a container of some kind. A small basket or box or bag will do. Soon it will be full to overflowing. From time to time look at what you wrote. No one can be discontent for long with so much to be thankful for."

In addition to filling a "blessing basket" on a daily basis, we could write a letter to God once a year, listing all that pours out of our hearts for his extravagant grace to us. Think of what a joy it would be to keep our annual letters of gratitude to read through the years or to pass on to our children.

Whether our "Thank yous" are momentary, intentional pauses in the midst of a hectic day, thank-you notes to God for his many blessings, or lengthy discourses of his grace, cultivating an attitude of gratitude will remind us of the truth that undergirds our lives: "For the LORD is good and his love endures forever; his faithfulness continues through all generations" (Ps. 100:5).

Enter his gates with thanksgiving and his courts with praise; give thanks to him and praise his name.

PSALM 100:4

Rejoice!

> The word grace emphasizes at one and the same time the
> helpless poverty of man and the limitless kindness of God.
> WILLIAM BARCLAY

I think it would be a good idea if you could lose a few pounds before the tour begins," my manager suggested gingerly.

Yeah, and I think it would be a good idea if you grew your hair back! I thought to myself.

Bill Latham meant well. I was going on the tour of a lifetime, supporting British megastar Cliff Richard. Cliff has never been well known in America, but in the rest of the world he has sold more singles than The Beatles, The Rolling Stones, and The Who all put together. (And no, those are not southern gospel quartets!) As well as being a successful pop star, Cliff is also a committed Christian. Once a year he would do a tour for a British relief charity called Tear Fund, and this time I was the opening act.

I was humiliated by Bill's "suggestion," but I'll admit I needed to lose weight. I don't mean I was huge. You couldn't have shown *Ben Hur* on my posterior, but I definitely fell into the "chunky" category. I had tried for ages to lose the twenty pounds that I tucked into my jeans and under my sweater; but they were clingy little pounds and reluctant to be evicted from their cozy, well-fed home.

"I've tried to diet," I whined pathetically. "My pastor told me that if I would just carry all of my diet books up and down the stairs a few times I'd never have a weight problem again."

"I have a plan," Bill said with a look of confidence.

My heart sank.

"I'm enrolling you in a clinic in London for two weeks. They will exercise you and put you on a strict diet and work wonders." He beamed. "You'll be a new woman!"

Good grief! I thought.

"All you have to do is stick with the program. Will you do that?"

"Oh, yes," I said with all the fervor of an alcoholic with a fifth of Scotch hidden in her sweater.

When I arrived at the "clinic" (i.e., fat farm), I was weighed in by a skinny thing who looked like her clothes had been sprayed on to emphasize her tiny frame. I had to keep my mouth firmly clamped so I wouldn't blurt out what was on the tip of my tongue: "Listen, Bones, if it wasn't for people like me, you'd be out of a job!"

For the next two weeks, Bones and her friends wrapped me and pummeled me and starved me till I looked like a leftover turkey at the homeless shelter on Thanksgiving. Then came D-Day. I think of it as "Black Tuesday." I stood on the scale and could have shot the little traitor. I had gained four pounds!

That's just one of the humiliating moments in my history. I hated myself. I was so ashamed that I had no willpower. I felt ugly and unlovable. I imagined when people looked at me they saw a fat, unattractive girl, because that's what I saw in the bathroom mirror . . . if I turned on the light.

But Christ didn't die so I'd continue to feel rotten about myself! Ephesians 2:13 tells me, "But now in Christ Jesus you who once were far away have been brought near through the blood of Christ." I spent many years as a believer, knowing I was pardoned for my sin but keeping a distance even from God because I didn't find myself worth loving. Every magazine I read showed images so far removed from my reality that I despaired of ever feeling worthy—until I was invited to a party with Cliff Richard and realized that all the so-called "beautiful people" were empty if they had no relationship with Christ. I sat and listened as Cliff shared his faith with people whose faces were well known to me. I watched as tears streamed down perfect makeup onto designer dresses. I realized how I had bought into the lies and despair of the world. I asked God to forgive me. I didn't need to be a "new woman" according to the world's ideas. I was already loved completely by God, as the woman I was.

When you look in a mirror, what do you see? Do you zero in on a crooked nose, a blemish, a sagging jaw, tired eyes packing their own bags? Have whole parts of your body moved to a new neighborhood? I encourage you as a fellow traveler to cherish and celebrate the gift of grace that calls you to draw near, to let go of your obsession with the shell of your life, and to fall more in love with Jesus. As women who have been drawn close to the heart of God by the embrace of Christ, you and I have the best reason of all to rejoice. Because God is near—no matter what.

Rejoice in the Lord always. I will say it again: Rejoice! . . . The Lord is near.

PHILIPPIANS 4:4–5

Hosanna the Donkey

Miss Dawn is my hero. Twice a week she takes care of a roaming pack of three-year-olds at Christ Presbyterian Academy's Toddler Time. She is smiling when we arrive at 9:10 A.M., and then, as if to serve as visual proof of the existence of God, she is still smiling at 2:15 P.M. when the day ends. Our son, Christian, loves her. When he prays for her at night he goes all mushy. What a gift from God when your child's first teacher is such a sweetheart.

Each time Christian gets out of school I check his lunch box to see if he has eaten any of his lunch. Usually he just rearranges it. Then I read his "What kind of day I had today" sheet. It's almost always the same:

> Christian had a good day today. He participated in everything and was very communicative [just like his dad]. He didn't eat much and didn't take his nap, but he lay quietly like a good boy, occasionally whispering to his rabbit, Whitey.

My desk is covered with things Christian has made at school. A manger made out of graham crackers. A tulip made from his handprint cut out of pink paper and folded in like petals. A jewelry box in the shape of a cross which he presented to me with the matter-of-fact statement, "Jesus died for your sins and this is for your rings." So I knew that during Easter week Miss Dawn was sharing more than just the Easter Bunny with her pint-size boys and girls.

My son, being a typical male, does not always give me all the information I'd like at the end of each school day. Still, I try.

"How was school today?"

"Fine."

"What did you learn?"

"Nothing."

"Did you sing?"

"No."

"Did you play outside?"

"No."

"So you just sat around for five hours and did nothing?"

"Did you say something, Mommy?"

I've learned that the best way to get Christian to "spill his stuff" is to go bike riding together. So every evening he and I mount up and head for the hills, and you wouldn't believe what I learn as we kick up dust together.

The evening before Good Friday we were pushing our bikes back into the garage when he said, "You know, Mom, today when I was Jesus riding into Jerusalem on a donkey, Tristan and Zachary waved branches to say hello. It was cool."

"You were Jesus?" I asked, wondering at Miss Dawn's discernment as she cast the roles.

"Sure! Hey, you want me to do it for Daddy and Papa?" he asked, full of joy at the thought of an encore performance.

We went inside and announced that the show was about to begin. That's not unusual in our household. We have frequent performances. Sometimes they're from *Mary Poppins* or *The Wizard of Oz*. This, however, was our first biblical epic. Christian and I hid behind the door leading into the kitchen where Barry and William, Christian's grandpa, waited in eager (?) expectation.

"Okay," Christian said. "I'll be Jesus and you be Hosanna."

"What do you mean?" I asked. "Who's Hosanna?"

"Well, the donkey, of course!" he said, looking at me as if I had temporarily backslidden.

"Why do you think the donkey's name is Hosanna?"

"Mommy, think about it. I'm Jesus, right?"

"Right."

"Well, as I'm coming in they all shout, 'Hosanna!' That's not me. That has to be you."

I tried to explain that "Hosanna!" is a cry of praise and adoration, that it was directed toward Jesus. He listened intently and then announced, "Okay, Hosanna. We're on."

As we reenacted that joyful scene in the Gospels, I thought about how dreadful it is that so many of those who exuberantly cried, "Hosanna to the One who comes in the name of the Lord!" also cried out, "Crucify him!" just a few days later. And I wonder if we as human beings have changed much in the two thousand years since those fickle cries sent Jesus to the cross. If you are like me, you often feel like two people. Some days we live in such a way that our actions cry out praise to God. But on other days it's as if we crucify Christ all over again.

The most wonderful thing about the love of God expressed in Christ is that none of this is a surprise to him. God entrusted his Son to a harsh, cruel world knowing that it would first embrace him and then spit on him and kill him. And yet he did it anyway—because his love has no limits. God's love cannot be quenched by the ever-turning tides of human emotion and devotion.

If I could say only one thing, it would be simple and to the point: God knows all about you. He knows your good days and your bad days. He knows the noble thoughts and the shameful thoughts. He sees your devotion and your indifference. And he loves you — totally, completely, passionately, boundlessly. Forever.

Oh the Passion, Oh the wonder,
Of the fiery love of Christ.
King of Glory on the altar. Perfect lamb of sacrifice.
Who are we that he would love us? Who but he
would give his life?
Oh the Passion, Oh the wonder,
Of the fiery love of Christ.
Oh the wisdom, Oh the wonder,
Of the power of the cross.
Love so rare no words could tell it. Life himself has
died for us.
Who are we that he would save us? Crucified to give
us life?
Oh the wisdom, Oh the wonder,
Of the power of the cross.

SHEILA WALSH

You are loved! You are loved passionately and unconditionally by the God who gave his only Son so you could rest secure in his eternal embrace.

They Call Me the Wanderer

I lost Lily again last night. It's the fourth time in a month. She hides in the linen closet or in the attic or under Christian's bed. The truth is, our cat, Lily, is a wanderer at heart.

I first saw her when she was in a little cage at the Nashville Humane Society. It was a weekend when Barry, William, and Christian were in Charleston, South Carolina, and I had stayed home to write. Barry and I have a kind of agreement that I won't visit the Humane Society by myself, but I don't find that agreement particularly binding. I try to avoid Harding Road, home of all waifs and strays, but when I'm by myself, it's hard.

That particular day I thought, *I'll just stop in and pet a few kitties and leave a donation for food and shelter.* Once I was there, however, something kicked in. I looked at all the cats in their cages looking so trapped and eager to be free. I scratched ears and sang little cat songs. Some stuck friendly paws through bars or purred like freshly tuned engines.

The only cat whose face I couldn't see was Lily's. She was sitting in her cage curled up in a basket, back to the world. I could tell that she was a beautiful cat. She was gold and white and had black markings on her long hair. I asked the attendant if I could take her out of her cage and hold her. I was told that I could at my own risk. I had no idea if she would bite me or throw up a hair ball on my new sweater. Instead she tucked her head under my arm and went to sleep.

Of course I took her home. I had two days to teach her the house rules before the boys returned. It was a piece of cake. She is the best cat in the world. She is more like a dog. She follows me everywhere I go. Barry was mad for a day, William was ecstatic, and Christian ran around the house crying out, "I have a sister! I have a sister!"

Lily's only little eccentricity is that she tends to wander. Most of the time I find her in one of her familiar hiding spots, but not last night. Everyone else was in bed. I was working late. So at about 2:00 A.M. I went to say good night to her before I turned in. No Lily. I looked everywhere. I checked all her usual camp-outs and came up empty.

After about an hour I knew she was not in the house. I got a flashlight and headed out into the backyard in my pajamas. Our house backs onto a golf course so there's a lot of ground to cover. I kept calling her name. "Lily! Lily! Where are you, you little monkey?" I knew I had to find her before morning. My neighbors have a gigantic Doberman pinscher, and Lily would be no more than a mid-morning snack to Lular.

After thirty minutes of calling her name, I heard a faint meow. I kept calling her and walking toward the sound until I found her, hiding behind a bush. I picked her up and carried her home. She almost rubbed a hole in my leg she was so grateful to be safe, to be inside, to be back on familiar ground.

I thought about that as I lay in bed having fed her a celebratory can of tuna fish. I thought, *God is like that.* We all have wandering hearts. We all hide in closets or under beds and occasionally get outside a safe place . . . and time after time, God comes looking for us. There is nowhere that you can hide that the boundless love of God can't find you. No matter what kind of mess you get into, he'll be there.

Lily's paws were muddy and my pajamas were covered in dirt. How much more does God allow himself to be covered in our mud, our sin, our messes? But you'll never hear a word of complaint. Just a "Welcome home, you little monkey!"

Perhaps you feel as if you have gone too far. Let me assure you, you cannot go too far from God. Remember the words of that wonderful hymn written by a father who had lost everything he loved, apart from God: "Oh love that will not let me go." Not "could not let me go" but "will not let me go."

So when you hear that quiet call in your spirit in the darkest night of your life when you are lost beyond belief, just let out a little meow . . . and God will find you and carry you home and wash you off and feed you. He will always celebrate your return.

Even when we cross every boundary, God's boundless love finds us. We are never lost to God.

Greyfriars Bobby

It was the middle of the nineteenth century. Queen Victoria was on the throne in London. To the north, many of the people in Scotland struggled to provide for their families. Those who lived off the land were perhaps the hardest hit of all. Bad weather, storms, and floods ruined crops and left entire families penniless and homeless, so they came to the larger cities looking for work.

One such man was John Gray. He arrived in Edinburgh in 1853 with his wife and only son. The situation there was no better. He became only one of many voices crying out for work and a place to sleep. The place he found was cold, damp, and miserable.

One bleak morning in January he got up before dawn, washed his face in cold water, and set off toward the large police station by Saint Giles Cathedral. He was stopped at the door and asked his business.

"I'd like to become a police officer," he said.

"How old are you?"

"I'm forty years of age," he replied.

"We're looking for men half your age, but if the doctor says that you are fit, you will do."

So John Gray became part of the Edinburgh police force. There were two requirements in his new position. One, he had to live in the area of the city that was to be his responsibility, and two, he had to have a watchdog. John found a six-month-old Skye terrier and named him Bobby.

It's hard to think of a Skye terrier as much of a watchdog. Its legs are barely six inches off the ground. It has long, silky hair that hangs over its eyes and a stumpy little tail. But Charles St. John, a famous nature writer in Scotland, wrote that Skye terriers are unusual in many ways. They will lie still for hours at a time. They will eat almost anything given to them. And one of their most peculiar traits, he says, is that they have a tendency to run on three legs as if keeping one on reserve for emergencies!

What John Gray found that day was a true friend for life. Bobby was a fiercely loyal, constant companion on the cold winter nights. Then John's health began to fail. He developed what was common in those days in Scotland: tuberculosis. The only cure was a warm climate or clean air. Edinburgh's air was neither warm nor pure. As a city it was referred to as Old Reekie because of the black soot that bellowed out of the chimney tops.

Bobby sat by his master's bed every day, hoping that he would recover. But in February of 1858, John Gray died. The little dog could not understand why his master was being placed in a wooden box. He followed the coffin to the Greyfriars churchyard and watched as it was placed in a hole in the ground.

John's widow picked up the little dog and took him home. That night Bobby cried and cried by the door until John's son finally let him out. The dog made his way back to Greyfriars Church and to the place where John was buried. He returned there every day. The family tried to make him stay in out of the cold air, but he would cry at the door until someone finally let him out.

John's grave became Bobby's home. He lived fourteen more years. John's widow and son moved on, but Bobby would not leave. There are many reports and photographs in old Scottish newspapers of the little dog whose loyalty and love for his master touched a whole city. If you were to visit Edinburgh today and you made your way to a street called Candlemakers Row, there you would find a statue of Bobby. A monument has been erected to this most unusual dog, now lovingly referred to as Greyfriars Bobby, the terrier who refused to leave his master's grave.

We are moved by this kind of loyalty. We all love to think that we could inspire in man or beast such a fierce devotion. But there is a far greater story than the tale of this dog. It is the story of the total dedication of the heart of God to you and me. If you pick up your Bible and scan the pages of human history, you'll find many common threads. There is the thread of the failure of men and women to live up to their commitments to God, and the failure of God to renege on any of his commitments to them. Such a stubborn love!

Give thanks to the LORD, for he is good;
his love endures forever.
Let the redeemed of the LORD say this—
those he redeemed from the hand of the foe,
those he gathered from the lands,
from east and west, from north and south.
Some wandered in desert wastelands,
finding no way to a city where they could settle.
They were hungry and thirsty, and their lives ebbed
    away.
Then they cried out to the LORD in their trouble,
and he delivered them from their distress.
He led them by a straight way
to a city where they could settle.
Let them give thanks to the LORD for his unfailing
    love
and his wonderful deeds for men,

for he satisfies the thirsty
and fills the hungry with good things.

PSALM 107:1–9

Six times in that psalm the phrase "unfailing love" is used. This is how God loves us. He will not give up on us nor leave our side. When we are strong, he walks with us. When we are weak, he sits with us. On our deathbed he is there to carry us home.

Stubborn love. Resolute, determined, eternal.

No matter where you are today, you are not alone. You are surrounded, undergirded, and guarded by the unfailing love of God.

Did You Eat Your Lunch?

It was the same deal every day. He prepared himself for it on the walk home from school. Ben and his friend Luke would kick the dusty road with their sandals until clouds formed over their heads, and they would cough and laugh and laugh and cough. Then Ben would rehearse, "Yes, Mom, I ate my lunch. No, Mom, I'm not kidding. Yes, Mom, every bite . . . and it was deeelicious!" When he got home, he knew his mom would laugh at that and make a poor attempt at swatting him with a towel.

It was a mystery to Ben and Luke why mothers felt obliged to be so obsessed with food.

"What I can't understand," Luke said, "is why my mom is always trying to stuff anything that's not moving into me when she hardly eats enough herself to keep a frog alive. I guess it's because Dad says her figure gets more like a pomegranate every day!"

They laughed at that thought as they parted for the day, Ben to one side of the hill, Luke to the other.

"See you tomorrow, Ben. Remember, my mom invited you over to play after school."

"I remember. Bye!"

When he got home, Ben knocked his shoes on the side of the house to shake off most of the sandy dust. "Mom,

I'm home!" he called as he went inside. "And I ate my lunch, in case you were wondering!"

Ben was a picky eater and small for his age, so Mary, like all good mothers, worried. "Well, I'm glad to hear it," she said with a smile as she swatted him with a towel.

The next morning as the sun streamed through the open kitchen window, Mary called, "Ben! Are you up yet?"

"Yeah, I'm up," he called back.

"Are you actually out of bed with both feet on the floor?" she asked.

How do mothers know that stuff? Ben wondered as he forced his right foot to join his left foot on the floor.

"I've packed you something special for lunch today," his mom said as Ben dragged his sleepy form into the kitchen. "It's one of your favorites: a couple of pickled fish and a few fresh-baked rolls, hot out of the oven."

"What's 'a few,' Mom?" Ben asked. "Enough to feed the whole school?"

"That's enough of that, young man, and I'll be checking your lunch box when you get home!"

"I'll be a little later today, Mom, remember? Luke's mom invited me over to play for a while."

"That's fine. Just remember your manners and be home before dinner."

As the afternoon shadows began to grow long over Luke's house later that day, Luke's mom said, "It's getting late, Ben. I think you should head home now. Don't forget your lunch box."

Lunch box! Ben thought. *Oh no, I forgot to eat my lunch! Well, maybe I'll meet a hungry dog on the way home.*

Ben wandered down the lane and headed toward the hill that stood between his house and Luke's. It was usually deserted at this time of afternoon, but there was a huge crowd ahead of him. Ben had never seen so many people. *I wonder what's going on?* he thought. He tried to see, but the crowd was too thick. He got down on his hands and knees and made his way through a maze of legs and robes and sandals until he got to the front where a man was talking.

Ben didn't recognize him, but his voice was like a waterfall, soothing and fresh. After a few moments the man stopped. Some of his friends were whispering in his ear. Ben watched their worried expressions. They seemed very cross.

I wonder if I'm going to get in trouble for pushing to the front? he thought, as one of the men came toward the crowd. Then Ben heard him ask if anyone had any food.

Oh great, this is better than giving it to a dog, Ben thought as he stood up to offer his slightly battered lunch. The man didn't seem entirely thrilled with the meager offering, but he took it anyway and gave it to the One who didn't seem worried at all. Ben watched this man named Jesus lift the little lunch up to the sky.

What's he doing with it? Ben wondered, wide-eyed. The crowd became very quiet.

> Taking the five loaves and the two fish and looking up to heaven, he gave thanks and broke the loaves. Then he gave them to his disciples to set before the people. He also divided the two fish among them all.
>
> MARK 6:41

Ben could not believe his eyes! He knew what he had in his lunch box. He had five of his mom's little rolls and two pickled fish, *little* pickled fish. But as he watched, this Jesus kept dividing it and dividing it and there was more and more and more. Jesus' friends began distributing the food to the crowd. Ben looked at the man beside him.

That one man seemed to have in his hands more bread and fish than Ben had in his lunch box to begin with! Everyone was eating his fill.

The number of the men who had eaten was five thousand.

MARK 6:44

Ben had some of the food too, and it tasted better than anything he could remember from his mom's kitchen. When it was all over and the people began to disperse, Ben watched as some of the men who were with Jesus gathered up baskets full of what was left over. There was enough to feed Ben's whole school for a week!

Wait till I tell Luke about this! he thought. *He'll never believe it.*

Ben hurried home, realizing that he was much later than he had told his mother he would be. He ran into the house.

"Mom! Mom! Where are you?"

"Where am *I*?" his mom said as she came out of the bedroom. "Where have *you* been, young man? Do you know what time it is? I was just about to walk over to Luke's house and fetch you back myself."

"But, Mom, I've got something to tell you!"

"It's a little late for that, kiddo. Go on upstairs and wash your face and hands. You look filthy. And what's that on the back of your robe? Have you been rolling on the grass again? How many times do I have to tell you about that!"

"But, Mom—"

"But nothing. Go on, now. And one more thing: Did you eat your lunch?"

Whatever you have today is enough. It might not look like it to you, but put into Jesus' hands, it is more than enough. It is lavish.

Is It Love . . .
or Is It the Flu?

Barry and I had been dating for over a year, and tonight we were going to one of our favorite Laguna Beach restaurants. Italian. Inside my size six or eight body (depending on the time of the month, new Ben and Jerry's ice-cream flavors, the situation in Bosnia, etc.), there is a robust Italian woman longing to get out.

I knew Barry would pick me up around 7:00, so I had just enough time to finish an essay for my C. S. Lewis class at Fuller Seminary. I was in no great rush. We were far beyond the trying-to-look-perfect-on-every-date stage. (That lasted about four dates for me . . . too much work.)

Next time I looked at the clock I saw it was almost seven. I changed out of my jeans and put on a dress. I'm not much of a dress woman. My favorite uniform is blue jeans, a white shirt, and no shoes. If I do wear shoes, then they usually have four-inch heels. I believe it goes back to my primal fear of God calling me to be a missionary in lands with great hairy beasties. In my subconscious mind I determined that if God was scanning the earth looking for good missionary stock he would say, "Well, we can't send her. Look at her shoes!" So although dresses are not my thing (I have fat knees—honestly!), I made some concessions for Barry.

At seven on the dot the doorbell rang. I opened the door, still struggling to get into shoe number two, and took a good look at my boyfriend.

"You don't look well," I said. "Are you feeling all right?"

"Yes! Sure! I'm fine," he replied, pacing the apartment like a woman with a wallet full of cash the day before Nordstrom's big sale.

"We don't have to go out," I said. "I could cook something and we could watch a movie."

"No! I mean . . . I'm fine. Really, I'm fine. Let's go."

It usually took fifteen minutes to drive from my apartment to downtown Laguna, but on a busy Friday night all bets were off. Barry seemed to be getting worse as we waited in traffic. I felt his forehead.

"You're hot," I said. "I think you might have the flu. It's going around, you know."

"Really, I promise I don't have the flu. I might throw up, but don't worry . . . I don't have the flu."

We finally found a parking spot and made our way into the bustling restaurant. Those innocents without reservations had no hope, but Barry had planned ahead. We were shown to our table and I remember thinking as I watched him sweat, *I wonder if he wants to break up with me? If he does, then I'm definitely having the tiramisu. Two of them!*

The waiter gave us our menus. I set mine down on the table for a moment, enjoying the boisterous Italian atmosphere.

"Aren't you going to order?" Barry barked.

"Man, you're cranky tonight," I said. "Here, have some bread. Your blood sugar must be low."

He glared at me. Finally, to avoid an international incident, I picked up my menu to look for the most fattening item. Cranky men do not deserve thin girlfriends.

I couldn't understand the menu at first. There wasn't a cream sauce in sight. Then I realized that it wasn't a menu at all, but a typed-out proposal.

I love you with all my heart. Will you marry me?

I stared at the words for a moment. Then I looked up and found myself staring into a television camera.

"Am I on *Candid Camera*?" I asked.

"Well, answer him!"

The voice came from behind me. It was my best friend, Marlene. I suddenly realized that the restaurant was full of our friends, all waiting for my answer.

I turned back to look at Barry, but he wasn't there. He was on his knees beside me holding out the most beautiful ring imaginable. There was a moment of silence. All eyes were on us.

"Yes," I answered. "Of course I will marry you." Everyone cheered and clapped.

Later that evening as Barry was dropping me off at my apartment I asked him, "What would you have done if I'd said no? I mean, you had a camera crew; all our friends were watching. It could have been mortifying!"

"You are worth the risk," he said simply as he kissed me good night.

I often think about that when I meet women across the country. One thing we all have in common is a deep desire for love that says, "You are worthwhile. You are priceless. You are worth risking for." We have a deep well that we long to have filled with significance and a sense of belonging. We want to be cherished.

I don't know how romantic your life is or how many sweet moments and memories you have tucked into the satin pockets of your heart. But I know this: you are adored and cherished by God. Human romance is wonderful, but it comes and goes. God's passionate love for us never wanes. It's not affected by whether we are size six or twenty-six. And the outlandish lengths to which God will go to prove his love are beyond any scheme a human being—even one as willing to risk as my husband—could dream up.

> This is how God showed his love among us: He sent his one and only Son into the world that we might live through him. This is love: not that we loved God, but that he loved us and sent his Son as an atoning sacrifice for our sins.
>
> 1 John 4:9–10

I'd say that's a pretty outlandish plan. What a risk he took! I mean, we could have all said, "No, thanks." And many have.

I'm so glad I said yes to God's invitation to an everlasting love. How about you?

Every time you look in the mirror, remember that you are treasured and loved by the ultimate Lover.

FAITH

Women of Faith partners with various Christian
organizations, including Zondervan,
Campus Crusade for Christ International,
Crossings Book Club, Integrity Music,
International Bible Society,
Partnerships, Inc., and World Vision
to provide spiritual resources for women.

For more information about Women of Faith
or to register for one of our nationwide conferences,
call 1-800-49-FAITH.

www.women-of-faith.com

Women of Faith Devotionals

Joy Breaks
Hardcover 0-310-21345-2

We Brake for Joy!
Hardcover 0-310-22042-4
Audio Pages® Abridged Cassettes 0-310-22434-9

OverJoyed!
Hardcover 0-310-22653-8
Audio Pages® Abridged Cassettes
0-310-22760-7

Extravagant Grace
Hardcover 0-310-23125-6
Audio Pages® Abridged
Cassettes 0-310-23126-4

Resources for Women of Faith^{SM}

BOOKS/AUDIO

The Joyful Journey	Hardcover	0-310-21344-4
	Softcover	0-310-22155-2
	Audio Pages® Abridged Cassettes	0-310-21454-8
	Daybreak	0-310-97282-5
Bring Back the Joy	Hardcover	0-310-22023-8
	Softcover	0-310-22915-4
	Audio Pages® Abridged Cassettes	0-310-22222-2
Outrageous Joy	Hardcover	0-310-22648-1
	Audio Pages® Abridged Cassettes	0-310-22660-0

WOMEN OF FAITH BIBLE STUDY SERIES

Celebrating Friendship 0-310-21338-X
Discovering Your Spiritual Gifts 0-310-21340-1
Embracing Forgiveness 0-310-21341-X
Experiencing God's Presence 0-310-21343-6
Finding Joy 0-310-21336-3
Growing in Prayer 0-310-21335-5
Knowing God's Will 0-310-21339-8
Strengthening Your Faith 0-310-21337-1

WOMEN OF FAITH WOMEN OF THE BIBLE STUDY SERIES

Deborah: Daring to Be Different for God 0-310-22662-7
Esther: Becoming a Woman God Can Use 0-310-22663-5
Hannah: Entrusting Your Dreams to God 0-310-22667-8
Mary: Choosing the Joy of Obedience 0-310-22664-3
Ruth: Trusting That God Will Provide for You 0-310-22665-1
Sarah: Facing Life's Uncertainties with a Faithful God 0-310-22666-X

WOMEN OF FAITH Zondervan*Groupware*™

Capture the Joy	Video Curriculum Kit	0-310-23096-9
	Leader's Guide	0-310-23101-9
	Participant's Guide	0-310-23099-3

*Inspirio's innovative and elegant gift books
capture the joy and encouragement that is an integral part
of the Women of Faith^{SM} movement.*

Joy for a Woman's Soul
Promises to Refresh Your Spirit
ISBN: 0-310-97717-7

Grace for a Woman's Soul
Reflections to Renew Your Spirit
ISBN: 0-310-97996-X

Simple Gifts
*Unwrapping the Special
Moments of Everyday Life*
ISBN: 0-310-97811-4

**Hope for a
Woman's Soul**
*Meditations to
Energize Your
Spirit*
ISBN: 0-310-98010-0

Padded Hardcover
4 x 7
208 pages

*Verses from the New International Version of
the Bible have been collected into these topically arranged volumes
to inspire Women of Faith^{SM} on their spiritual journey.*

Prayers for a Woman of Faith^{SM}
ISBN: 0-310-97336-8

**Words of Wisdom
for a Woman of Faith**^{SM}
ISBN: 0-310-97390-2

**Promises of Joy
for a Woman of Faith**^{SM}
ISBN: 0-310-97389-9

**Words of Wisdom
for a Woman of Faith**^{SM}
ISBN: 0-310-97735-5

**Psalms and Proverbs
for a Woman of Faith**^{SM}
ISBN: 0-310-98092-5

**Promises of Love
for a Woman of Faith**^{SM}
ISBN: 0-310-98249-9

Hardcover
5-1/4 x 5-1/4
128 pages